PRAISE FOR DESPERATE FOR JESUS . . .

"All believers need this book! Thank you, John Hannah, for so candidly sharing your story and doing what you do best—bringing people to Jesus Christ. We must be desperate to know Him like the psalmist. In his deep thirst, his soul panted for the living waters. Our souls must thirst for Him. The path you lay out in this book to bring us to that place where we run to living waters is life-changing. All who are quenched with the Living Water will thirst no more."

—REVEREND KENETY S. GEE

senior pastor, Chatham Fields Lutheran Church, Chicago
and president/CEO of Chicago Global Health Alliance

"In this book, Pastor Hannah shares personal and profound stories from his life, inspiring us not simply to seek an experience with God, but also an encounter with Him. Thoroughly woven with Scripture and personal stories, *Desperate for Jesus* encourages believers to perform an evaluation of self, spirit, and sacrifice. Thank you, Pastor Hannah, for not only reminding us to remain desperate for Jesus, but also guiding us to that place."

—PASTOR ERIC HAMPTON

Arrow Church, Chicago Heights, Illinois

"*Desperate for Jesus* is full of inspiration and wisdom! Pastor Hannah reminds us that there will be days our faith will waver:

'When you can't pray, surround yourself with prayer warriors. When you can't stand, surround yourself with people who'll stand for you and with you.' In those times, surrounding ourselves with prayer support is crucial; it can ultimately determine our outcome. I thank God for this book. It will encourage, empower, and give greater insight into your Christian journey!"

—PASTOR CLIFTON HURT
Chayil Advancing Life Ministries, Chicago, Illinois

"I understand that God has given me a platform, and that my job is not to hoard that platform but to bring young men and women of leadership onto that platform. John Hannah wasn't looking for a platform. But because of his audacious, blind faith, his desperation for God's presence, and his willingness to meet people where they live, God has prepared and blessed him. It's phenomenal what he's accomplishing in Chicago. He is part of something God is doing that is much bigger than any of us. And it's time his story of desperation for Jesus—and all the obstacles we face in pursuit of Him—reaches beyond church walls to where people really live."

—WILFREDO "CHOCO" DE JESÚS
senior pastor, New Life Covenant Church in Chicago *and author of* In the Gap *and* Amazing Faith

"I love what my friend John Hannah says about finding true life in *Desperate for Jesus.* If anyone can speak on being desperate for Jesus, it's John. I've known him for seventeen years now and have witnessed his amazing journey as God has blessed him to pastor one of the fastest-growing churches in our nation. Over the course of that journey, John's passion and desperation for our Savior has not diminished one bit. In fact, it has only grown stronger. His humility, transparency, and love for God and His people are apparent throughout this book as John candidly shares his story and what it looks like to live desperate for Jesus, In these pages, he offers a gift for the body of Christ. Well done!"

—PASTOR AJ JONES
City of Hope Church, Bolingbrook, Illinois

"Pastor Hannah, wow! Thank you for your vision, passion, and strength for this generation and this gift to them. Your story is inspiring and will no doubt empower young people to live desperate for Jesus."

—PASTOR ANDRE GROSS
Assembly of Faith Outreach Center, Chicago, Illinois

"Most Christians desire a deep, meaningful, and transforming relationship with Jesus, but many aren't sure about how to get it. In *Desperate for Jesus,* John Hannah brilliantly brings Scripture to life as he draws from his own personal story to help us confront and overcome every challenge that keeps us from experiencing the fullness of God's story in our lives. This is a must-read book for anyone seeking a more practical, powerful, and personal relationship with God."

—REVEREND SHAUN DOUGLAS MARSHALL
senior pastor, Community Covenant Church, Calumet Park, Illinois

"Knowing Pastor John Hannah personally over the last three years as my mentor, I know this is a man who is in fact desperate for Jesus—still. In this book, he discusses personal struggles, seasons, and situations that have shaped him into the godly man he is today. However, these obstacles are not what have made him desperate for Jesus. Rather *because* Pastor Hannah is desperate for his Savior, he has overcome hard times. You will too. For anyone struggling with the problems and issues that life inevitably brings, this book is for you!"

—PASTOR D. BRANDON CAMPBELL ("PASTOR BCAM")
The City of Abundant Life Church, Chicago, Illinois

"I have known Pastor John Hannah for years and have enjoyed the opportunity and privilege to watch his life from behind the scenes. I can honestly say there is no greater role model for showing us what it looks like to be desperate for Jesus. I absolutely recommend this masterpiece and manual that many pastors and saints will follow. Love you, man of God."

—PASTOR CALVIN E. WATKINS
St. John Community Church, Robbins, Illinois

"What does it mean to live a life that's desperate for Jesus? John Hannah exemplifies the answer to that question. His personal walk with Christ has embodied the lessons illustrated within the pages of this book, and through the stories of Moses, Joseph, and David he introduces us to proven strategies that will help us live desperate for Jesus and overcome any obstacles we face. Thank you, John, for the wisdom you've shown us in this book."

—PASTOR CURTIS HILL

The City of Abundant Life Church, Chicago, Illinois,
and president of smallchurchbranding.com

DESPERATE
FOR JESUS

OVERCOME THE OBSTACLES
TO FIND TRUE LIFE

JOHN F. HANNAH

SALUBRIS
RESOURCES

Published by Salubris Resources
1445 N. Boonville Ave.
Springfield, Missouri 65802
www.salubrisresources.com

Cover design by PlainJoe Studios (www.plainjoestudios.com)
Interior design and formatting by Prodigy Pixel (www.prodigypixel.com)

Unless otherwise specified, all Scripture quotations are taken from the Holy
Bible, New International Version®, NIV®. Copyright © 1973, 1978, 1984, 2011 by
Biblica, Inc. ™ Used by permission of Zondervan. All rights reserved worldwide.
www.zondervan.com. The "NIV" and "New International Version" are trademarks
registered in the United States Patent and Trademark Office by Biblica, Inc.™

Scripture quotations from The MESSAGE, copyright by Eugene H. Peterson 1993, 1994,
1995, 1996, 2000, 2001, 2002. Used by permission of Tyndale House Publishers, Inc.

Scriptures marked (ESV) are from the ESV® Bible (The Holy Bible, English
Standard Version®), copyright © 2001 by Crossway, a publishing ministry
of Good News Publishers. Used by permission. All rights reserved.

Scripture quotations marked (NLT) are taken from the Holy Bible, New Living Translation,
copyright © 1996, 2004, 2007 by Tyndale House Foundation. Used by permission of
Tyndale House Publishers, Inc., Carol Stream, Illinois 60188. All rights reserved.

Scripture quotations marked (NASB) are taken from the New American Standard
Bible®, copyright © 1960, 1962, 1963, 1968, 1971, 1972, 1973, 1975, 1977, 1995 by
The Lockman Foundation. Used by permission. (www.Lockman.org)

Scripture quotations marked (KJV) are taken from King James
Version of the Bible, which is held in public domain.

Scripture quotations marked (NKJV) are taken from the New King James Version®.
Copyright © 1982 by Thomas Nelson. Used by permission. All rights reserved.

NOTE: Some of the names in this book, as well as some identifying details,
have been changed to protect the anonymity of the people involved.
ISBN: 978-1-68067-048-6
Printed in the United States of America
18 17 16 15 ● 1 2 3 4

———————————

This book is dedicated to my evangelist, *the late Pastor Allie Trimuel, who left everything to come with me and start New Life Church Southeast. She prayed for me, fasted for me, and was there every time I needed an ear. Words could never express how much you mean to me and* how much I miss you. *Forever in my heart . . .*

———————————

CONTENTS

FOREWORD

first met my "brother from another mother," John Hannah, more than twenty years ago when we came together to do a big youth event in Humboldt Park, here in Chicago. He impressed me as a passionate leader who was very committed to young people.

By the time he came to New Life Church, John was already well known as a powerful evangelist and preacher in the African-American church. Ours was a predominately Hispanic congregation, and a small one at that, so it came as a bit of a surprise that he felt called to come under our ministry. There were some definite obstacles to overcome, such as the ethnicity challenges and the shift from being an evangelist to becoming a shepherd. But John believed the Lord was leading him to New Life, and there was never a question that he wouldn't follow God's promptings.

John was the first African American to preach in our pulpit, and his gifting was undeniable. The illustrative way he preached the Word of God was unlike anything our people had seen or heard before. He opened his mouth, and people were moved. For four years under the leadership here, John continued in his role as an evangelist, speaking here some Sundays, preaching away on other Sundays. But I sensed something was missing in his ministry, something he couldn't continue without.

One Sunday John said to me, "I surrender to your authority. You do as you see fit." (John shares a detailed account of this story in the book—trust me, it's good!) At that point, I told him,

"John, I'm not threatened by your gift or by who you are. But I'm not going to plant you in ministry until you get a pastor's heart. Right now, you have an evangelist's heart. The evangelist drops the bomb, and then he leaves. But a pastor stays and shepherds and helps clean the wounds of a broken family."

And that was the beginning of a desperate year for John, twelve months of serving the poor and homeless in our area. Every Thursday for a year, he came from the South side of Chicago to make sandwiches and feed the hungry. What I thought would happen did happen. John began to see the face of Jesus in the eyes of those homeless men, and the trajectory of his ministry, his vision, changed. That experience shaped him into a shepherd, a man who was desperate to be in the presence of God and desperate to feed God's people.

That year broke John Hannah in the sense that he saw God in a whole different way. I told him, "John, this is where God wants us, among the people. We can never stop smelling like sheep. No matter how big we get, we've got to continue to smell like sheep."

And John Hannah smells like sheep. You see him with the people all the time. You see him hugging them. He attracts people who are perhaps in despair and loss because they see in him a sense of hope. John came from the inner city. He grew up in a drug-infested community, got his education, and did what so few who have a choice ever do: he stayed. Here's this completely humble, approachable guy who is immensely talented and anointed, and he's making it—in the inner city. He shops here. He works out in the gym here. And he still gives back to the city. He's faithful with what God has given him. Not only does he lead a large church, but also he has credibility because he genuinely cares about the people. And he can relate to them because he has been there. He even worked as a parole officer in Cook County, giving him further insight. John relates to, understands, and loves the people he serves.

As pastors, we live with a sense of urgency. We live in a state of tension, with needs, tragedies, and desperate situations all around us. You simply can't be a pastor and be nonchalant about what's happening around you. We desperately want to make sure that people come to know Jesus and are desperate to know Him intimately.

With that mission in sight, John and I have developed a relationship of accountability. Because we understand where we both are, and we want to steward what God has given us, we stay in constant communication. We constantly hold each other accountable, checking up on each other's marriages. The reality is that you can be desperately seeking God and desperately leading people to Him while your family and your marriage suffer in silence.

We have come to depend on each other in that way. The Lone Ranger needed Tonto. Batman needed Robin. John looks out for me, and I'm always looking out for him. That's the kind of relationship God has given us. And as a result we're both better men and better ministers of the gospel.

I understand that God has given me a platform, and that my job is not to hoard that platform but to bring young men and women of leadership onto that platform.

John wasn't looking for a platform. He was never desperate to be known. But because of his audacious, blind faith, his desperation for God's presence, and his willingness to meet people where they live, God has prepared and blessed him. He was not meant for the sideline. He was sent here to be at the forefront of everything. And now he is. It's phenomenal what he's accomplishing in Chicago. He is part of something God is doing that is much bigger than us. And it's time his story of desperation for Jesus—and all the obstacles we face in pursuit of Him—reaches beyond church walls to where people really live . . . because that's where John Hannah shines brightest.

—WILFREDO "CHOCO" DE JESÚS
senior pastor, New Life Covenant Church in Chicago and author of In the Gap *and* Amazing Faith

INTRODUCTION

The day just felt different. For years, he had come to this spot, had stationed himself and listened intently for the footsteps of people passing by. Some days were better than others. At times, people took pity on him and pitched a few coins his way. Others spit at and mocked him, blaming his infirmity on his sins or the sins of his parents.

There were no good days.

But on this day, the air was electric. The sound of footsteps was louder than usual. The voices of travelers were excited, infused with a sense of anticipation.

"What's happening?" he anxiously asked someone in the crowd, and quickly learned that Jesus of Nazareth was passing by. *Can it be? He who heals is near?*

Immediately, the blind beggar called out in his darkness, "Jesus, Son of David, have mercy on me!" only to hear shouts back from the crowd, rebuking him. "Be quiet!" they yelled. But Bartimaeus didn't let their scolding get to him. Instead, he shouted out all the more, "Son of David, have mercy on me!"

You may know the rest of his story. Upon hearing Bartimaeus' desperate cries, Jesus, the Messiah who several days later would die for all of humanity, stopped in His tracks and ordered the man to be brought to Him.

> When he came near, Jesus asked him, "What do you want me to do for you?"
>
> "Lord, I want to see," he replied.

Jesus said to him, "Receive your sight; your faith has healed you." Immediately he received his sight and followed Jesus, praising God. When all the people saw it, they also praised God. (Luke 18:40–43)

What Desperation Looks Like

My guess is that anyone could take one look at Bartimaeus and know this guy had lived a hard life. Who knows how long he had woken up in darkness, gone to the same spot, and begged for alms day after day—holding his breath for the response. Would it be the clink of a coin? Loud jeers and callous comments? Or even the wet spit of a stranger disgusted by his "sin"?

So when some told him that this Jesus of Nazareth he had heard about—the one who healed—was unexpectedly near, Bartimaeus called out to get Jesus' attention. Even when the crowd tried to silence him, he shouted at the top of his lungs. He wouldn't be shut up. He knew he was sitting on a once-in-a-lifetime opportunity. Bartimaeus was a desperate man.

Have you ever felt this way? Have you ever come to a place of hopelessness, feeling as if your life is leading nowhere? Human effort has failed you, and you're at your last resort, fully aware that only God can help you. Bartimaeus was at his last resort. I read this passage and think, *Now, that's desperation!* Obviously, the flesh had failed this man. He knew He needed Jesus' touch on his life. He was desperate to reach the one who could give him sight. He needed an encounter with the living God.

DESPERATION WILL MAKE YOU BEG.

In Mark 5, we read about Jairus, whose daughter was seriously ill. Jairus is an important man in the community. Part of the college of elders who managed every Jewish synagogue, he had social clout and power, But his civic influence carried no weight now. He knew He needed Jesus' touch on his daughter. He fell at Jesus' feet, pleading with Him, "My little daughter is dying. Please come and put your hands on her so that she will be healed and live" (Mark 5:23). Jairus was desperate for Jesus to come to his house. Human efforts had failed. Jesus agreed to come to his home, but on the way messengers came and said, "Don't bother the Teacher. Your daughter is now dead." Jesus turned to Jairus and said, "Do not be afraid; only believe" (Mark 5:36, NKJV). In desperation, Jairus continued to walk. Basically, Jesus was going to follow Jairus until he told Him to stop. Essentially, Jesus said, "If you keep walking towards your house, I'll follow you."

DESPERATION WILL MAKE YOU FORGE AHEAD IN HOPE.

As Jesus walked toward Jairus' house, a woman who had hemorrhaged for twelve years interrupted the parade of people. Everything had failed her. She had spent all she had on medical treatments, and her health had not gotten any better (Mark 5:25–26). In fact, her condition was worse. Her illness had crippled her not only physically, but emotionally and perhaps spiritually, as well. Because Jewish law declared her unclean, she was forbidden to enter the temple for religious ceremonies. According to Jewish law, anyone she touched or who touched her became unclean as well (Lev. 15:25–27). She lived as an outcast from society.

But now, Jesus was near, and she no longer cared about the risks. Scripture says she "pressed into" the crowd. *If I can just touch the hem of His garment,* she thought. Notice she wasn't walking. She didn't say, "If I could just touch His sleeve." She had to touch the hem. She actually crawled on the ground, willing to be stomped on and kicked, determined and hoping for a touch from Jesus. She was desperate for a miracle.

DESPERATION WILL MAKE YOU CRAWL.

I was in my mid-thirties when the time came for me to leave the church where I was serving. Desperation had set in, and I sensed the Lord saying to me like He said to Abraham when He called him: "Go from your country, your people and your father's household to the land I will show you" (Gen. 12:1). I remember taking my wife, Anna, by the hand and leaving everyone I loved so dearly. I didn't know where we were going. I just knew we had to leave. I asked God, *Where am I going?* and He showed me I was to go to Pastor Wilfredo "Choco" De Jesús' church, New Life Covenant Church, on the north side of Chicago.

I was familiar with the church and the pastor. When I organized youth conferences for the kids of inner-city Chicago, I met Choco, a youth leader at one of the churches that partnered with us, and we became quick friends. But still, why would God send me to a Puerto Rican church on the north side of Chicago, totally opposite from anything I knew? The church didn't sing the songs I was used to, and the preacher certainly didn't preach the way I was used to hearing the Word of God taught. The people were completely different. My wife and I were the only black people there. In my mind, it didn't seem logical.

DESPERATION WILL DRIVE YOU TO PLACES WITH NO UNDERSTANDING OF WHY AND WHERE YOU'RE GOING.

I went there and asked Choco, "Let me just come in and sit." And I sat. After a while, he anointed me as one of the pastors of the church. One Sunday morning, he and I were doing what's called a dual sermon—where he would preach, then I would preach, and we'd go back and forth. A little background: At this point in my life and in my ministry, I was serving in this church but interviewing for senior leadership positions at other churches. I was the definition of impatient, beyond frustrated that I wasn't leading a church yet.

So Choco and I were preaching on Moses, and we had this staff in our hands, talking about how only when Moses submitted his staff to God was God able to use him. I was preaching, and I sensed the Holy Spirit tell me, *Lay the staff at Choco's feet. And that means you're submitting to his authority.*

I was standing there thinking, *Nah, not going to happen.* Toward the end of the sermon, I looked at Choco and said, "Isn't it amazing that we—you and I—are standing here together? Isn't it amazing that God has brought me from the south side to the north side of the city to sit with you?" And I took the staff and laid it at his feet before God and everyone. I got on my knees in front of his whole church and said, "From this day forward, I lay my anointing, my gifts, and my talent at your feet, and I submit to your authority."

Make no mistake. My flesh didn't want to do it. We'll talk more in chapter 8 about how our flesh can be such an obstacle in our desperation for Jesus, but for now I just want to point out that desperation is a life of consistent submission. It will put you in a place where you're listening to people you would never have listened to before, and submitting when you thought you never would bow.

DESPERATION WILL MAKE YOU SUBMIT TO WHATEVER YOUR FLESH IS FIGHTING.

A word of caution here about submission. When you submit to someone, make sure they won't abort what God has put in you. Think of the wisdom of David. He submitted to King Saul until a jealous spirit got hold of Saul, and then David fled for his life. Unfortunately, desperation can lead us to people who dismantle instead of validate or enhance our calling. I knew I could trust Choco. I didn't have to worry about him. He told me, "I see what's in you, and it doesn't scare me; neither does it intimidate me. I want to *plant* it. I want to see it grow."

Choco trusted me. He let me preach. He let me teach. And in 2011, New Life Covenant Church planted New Life Covenant Southeast.

We've all felt desperation in our lives. It may not be desperation for Christ, but you know when you're at a desperate place. You're restless, discontent. You won't settle. When you're in a desperate place, you don't unpack. You care less about what people think or what they say. Like Bartimaeus, you literally have an I-don't-care attitude.

Bartimaeus wanted his sight. Jairus implored Jesus for healing. The bleeding woman crawled to Jesus for relief. I needed direction. What are your issues? What makes you desperate for Jesus?

Who Is Your Jesus?

Notice the words Bartimaeus used when he called out to Jesus: "Son of David, have mercy on me." At that time in ancient Israel, to call someone "Son of David" was a title equivalent to calling someone "Messiah," signifying to the Jews a person who was the promised descendant of King David and would sit upon the throne of Israel (2 Sam. 7:11–16). Bartimaeus got it! Other beggars asked Jesus for mercy, but Bartimaeus called out, "Son of David," indicating his faith in Jesus as his Messiah. They were the same words the crowds would shout only a few days later during Jesus' triumphal entry into Jerusalem (Matt. 21:9):

> The crowds that went ahead of him and those that followed shouted, "Hosanna to the Son of David!"
> "Blessed is he who comes in the name of the LORD!"
> "Hosanna in the highest heaven!"

Bartimaeus was desperate for Jesus. I wonder: if we really believed that Jesus is our Lord and Savior—that in Him we live, move and have our being (Acts 17:28), that Jesus, Himself, is the way, the truth, and the life (John 14:6)—would we be more desperate for His touch on our lives?

We often have distorted ideas of God and who Jesus is. Who is Jesus to you? Is He like a magic lamp you rub when you want something? Your hero when you get it; your excuse when you don't? Is He the one you run to when things go wrong, yet out of the picture when life is smooth? Is it possible that the Jesus you trust in is a counterfeit and not the true Jesus of the Bible? Is it possible that you aren't desperate for Him because you don't really know the Jesus that Bartimaeus, Jairus, and the bleeding woman knew and trusted with their lives?

Is your Jesus the Messiah, who only a few days after giving Bartimaeus his sight, resurrecting Jairus's daughter, and healing a social outcast, took on our sins on the cross? Is your Jesus the One who three days later rose from the dead to bring dead souls to life, to give peace that transcends all understanding, strength in the face of our adversity, and comfort in the midst of our storms? Is your Jesus a Jesus you're desperate to know and to know better?

What's Keeping You From Finding True Life?

When we pursue the real Jesus, we want to know the depths of His love. But often times, things get in the way of that pursuit. The obstacles seem insurmountable. Whether it's hard times in life, relationships, betrayal, anger, spiritual immaturity, or human desires, we can get blindsided by the things coming at us and lose or stall our desperation for Jesus. I often say that when we lose our pursuit, these obstacles keep us from seeing and finding true life, or as John 10:9–10 (ESV) calls it, *abundant life:*

> I am the door. If anyone enters by me, he will be saved and will go in and out and find pasture. The thief comes only to steal and kill and destroy. I came that they may have life and have it abundantly.

Did you catch that? Jesus tells us that through Him we have abundant life—that as the good shepherd He is the door to true life, a shelter from our spiritual Enemy, Satan.

To truly know the depths of Jesus' love and power, sometimes we have to walk through the fire—the difficult obstacles a broken world brings, or that we bring on ourselves by our choices. But always remember that through the fire, through your desperation, Jesus walks with you and brings you closer to Him as a result. When we stay focused on Jesus, we can lean into Him as we're purified and refined. The refinement process in ancient times (and still practiced today) gives us insight into how God redeems trials and obstacles in our lives to bring us closer to Him.

Stage 1: The craftsman breaks up the hardened rock filled with common minerals and possibly precious metals like gold and silver.

Stage 2: The craftsman puts the broken-up ore into a melting pot (called a crucible) that's able to withstand extreme heat temperatures, sometimes in excess of one thousand degrees Celsius, and then places the crucible into the furnace at the specific temperature necessary for removing other metals that mar the quality of the gold or silver.

Stage 3: The impurities are then removed. As the craftsman carefully watches the ore melt, he stirs the pot and skims off the layer of impurities called "dross" that rises to the top of the molten metal. Scripture talks about dross: "Remove the dross from the silver, and a silversmith can produce a vessel" (Prov. 25:4).

Stage 4: The craftsman turns up the heat and places the crucible back into the furnace, often up to as many as seven times. As the process is repeated, impurities are continually released to the surface.

Stage 5: The purification process continues as the dross is removed, gradually revealing precious silver. The craftsman gauges the progress by looking for his reflection on the surface of the silver-filled crucible. The more dross that's removed, the less distorted his reflection will be.

Stage 6: When the craftsman looks into the crucible and sees a clear reflection, the refining process is complete. The degree of purity is at its highest point.[1]

Hopefully, understanding the process of refining ore into precious treasure will help you understand the refinement process of what can feel like decades of trials and obstacles in your own life. Ultimately, God, the craftsman, redeems our trials, removing the impurities that keep us from the true, abundant life waiting to be revealed when we live desperate for Jesus. Ultimately, we become a reflection of Christ.

Three Sustaining Disciplines

Throughout the pages of this book, I've included tools to help you stay focused on Jesus and desperate for Him. In my own life, when I'm facing the fire, three things sustain me:

- prayer
- staying in God's Word
- the community/people I surround myself with in life and ministry

We'll dive headfirst into these in the next chapter, but I want to quickly tell you that prayer, Scripture, and people have made the difference in keeping me desperate for more of Jesus—regardless of the obstacles.

Believe it or not, we do have a God who knows us and wants us to know Him. I know it may not seem like that sometimes when the fires are threatening or raging, but you can be absolutely sure that God desperately wants you to know Him—to know His Word, to know His promises, and to know His heart. In the book of Acts, Luke wrote:

> His purpose was for the nations to seek after God and perhaps feel their way toward him and find him—though he is not far from any one of us. For in him we live and move and exist. As some of your own poets have said, "We are his offspring." (Acts 17:27–28, NLT)

I like that thought—that I'm God's offspring, that He knows me as His son, and that He wants me to know Him as my heavenly Father. He is desperate for me to overcome the obstacles that keep me from knowing Him intimately. So He walks with me through them, to help me know Him better and to come alongside others. Notice that through the whole refining process, the craftsman never leaves. He continually watches over the crucible, ensuring the end result. God doesn't leave us in our trials—the very opposite. He is always present, guarding His workmanship.

How do we get to the place where we're experiencing true life? Where, like Bartimaeus, our desperation for Jesus and our faith in Him as Messiah overcomes all obstacles, shame, and embarrassment? Are you ready for His promises to manifest in your life? Is it time to evaluate how you're spending your time, where you're putting your energies, who or what might be influencing you? Is it time to come closer to Jesus through prayer, His Word, and the godly people He's placed in your path? Then let's begin a journey together that's guaranteed to be life-changing. Let's find out what it means to live lives that are desperate for Jesus.

PART 1

A DESPERATE CHASE

CHAPTER 1

THE PLACE OF DESPERATION

'm often asked, "How do you get to that place in your life where you're desperate for Jesus?" My answer is straight and to the point: "You won't get there unless you have an encounter with Jesus." Religion won't get you to that place. Other people's faith won't get you there. I can talk all day, but until you have that personal encounter with Him, you won't know who the real Jesus is. Only when we encounter Him as our Lord and Savior do we become desperate to know Him better.

I was raised in church. My grandmother was the spiritual pillar of our house. But I saw a lot of life before my encounter with God. Both parents were high school dropouts. My mother got pregnant with me at age sixteen or seventeen, and I was born into poverty. Growing up in the Chicago projects, drugs were part of our community. Talk about passing on generational curses—

my father had gone to prison, but when he got out, I visited him on the weekends. He kept marijuana around the house and even taught me to smoke it when I was a kid. As I got older, things only got worse. I did all the radical things the kids around me did—smoked, abused drugs, partied.

I know what it's like to be desperate for an encounter with Jesus both in my own life and in the lifeless church I grew up in. Each weekend at church was the same. We stood up to sing, sat down to listen to the preacher, went to church at noon, came out at 2 o'clock—the whole time I felt as if we were all just going through the motions. It was ritual religion. The same people came in, and the same people went out. No transformation ever took place. I remember thinking *You can't tell me this is it. There must be more than this. Surely, this whole church and God-thing is bigger than what I'm seeing.* I wanted to see people saved and see the stories in the Bible come to life. I wanted to see fire come down, to see people being delivered. I couldn't take it.

I was desperate for Jesus and didn't even know it.

Experience vs. Encounter

When I was a kid, we used to play this game called "It." If you were "It," you had to chase someone and tag them, and then they were "it." Then it would be your turn to be chased. In many ways, my encounter with Jesus resembled a game of "It."

I was seventeen in my senior year of high school when, during a Wednesday night choir practice, God chased me and tagged me in the basement of that church I grew up in. Hands lifted up, saying, "Yes, Lord," I just found myself alone in the corner of the room weeping. All my life, I had asked for something deeper, I had grown more and more desperate for something else, and now God was answering, bringing me from shallow shores into deep waters with Him. I walked home, still weeping, went into my room, closed the door, got down on my knees and said the sinner's prayer, asking Jesus to come into my life. It was almost like God was saying to me, *Okay, now it's your turn. I've chased you. I've covered you, I've shielded you, but now it's your time to come to Me. You're "it."*

That night, I encountered Jesus as my Savior. Jesus says He draws us to Himself: "And I, when I am lifted up from the earth, will draw all people to myself" (John 12:32). Isaiah reminds us that His ear is not too heavy that He cannot hear us, that His hand is not too short that it cannot save us (Isa. 59:1).

That's the difference between an experience and an encounter. When you encounter God, it's personal, strictly between you and Him. You can go to church every Sunday and have an experience. You can sing, clap, and listen to the preacher. But nothing can compare to a personal encounter with Jesus. Once He touches you—once He calls you—nothing else matters.

I always think of the Israelites wandering in the desert of the Sinai Peninsula, telling Moses, "We want to talk to God ourselves. We're tired of talking to Him through you." And Moses said, "Okay, c'mon! Come to the mountain!" He knew that when they got to Mount Sinai, they would experience God for themselves and their lives would be changed.

When Jesus first walked by Peter, He looked at Peter and said, "Drop your net; I'll make you a fisher of men." Peter dropped his net into the water, saw it fill with fish, and from that point on walked with Jesus. Now *that's* an encounter! Peter was desperate for something more. I think about that song lyric based on Psalm 42. Though we don't know the psalm's author, some scholars believe David was likely the author who penned the psalm during the rebellion that his son, Absalom, led against him.

> As the deer panteth for the water
> So my soul longeth after you
> You alone are my heart's desire
> And I long to worship you.[1]

Once you have that encounter with Jesus, your life is changed forever—F-O-R-E-V-E-R. *Forever.*

That's why the local church and preaching the gospel are so necessary. The church is such a powerful entity. The moment someone walks through the door of a church, we have a responsibility to make sure they have an encounter with Jesus, not an experience. *Everyone* should have the opportunity to feel like Peter and David felt.

When I first planted my church, the Lord told me, *Your assignment is to introduce people to the glory, to Me.* As a shepherd, I'm to bring people into the presence of God so they can have that personal encounter. Once I preach, I tell God, "Okay, here they are. Do what You do."

If you've encountered Jesus, your encounter with Him likely looked different from mine or anyone else's, for that matter. It might have happened in church, on the side of the road, or in a hospital. You may have been alone (like I was) or in a sea of people. Your encounter may have been charged with emotion. Perhaps it was extremely calm. We're all wired differently—part of the plan of the Creator who knows us intimately. In fact, Luke 12:7 says that the one who made us knows the number of hairs on our heads: "Indeed, the very hairs of your head are all numbered. Don't be afraid; you are worth more than many sparrows."

Rest assured, He will draw you to Himself in a significant way that resonates with you. Everyone's path and encounter is different, but all roads lead to one place—one person—and that's Jesus Christ.

The Chase Begins

From the day I encountered Jesus, I began to chase after Him, desperate to really know Him. God touched me and said, "Now you're "It." And I've been chasing Him ever since. Early on, I knew I wanted to know Jesus in a deep way. I wanted relationship, not the religion I had grown up with. Until then, all I had known was my grandmother's God and the God of my denomination. I wanted to know the God of John Hannah. Suddenly, it was personal. When you come to know the true Jesus, you want to chase after Him.

When you come to know the true Jesus, you want to chase after Him.

Once you've had that encounter with Jesus, how do you chase after Him in ways that compel you to desperation for a deep, abiding relationship with Him? After encountering Him, all of this was new to me—my desire not to sin, not to walk according to fleshly desires, not to do the things I knew God wasn't pleased with. My whole desire, my cravings, had changed. Everything was foreign, everything, that is, except prayer.

CHASING AFTER GOD IN PRAYER

Having been raised in church by a praying grandmother, I knew about prayer. Down through the years, I had heard my grandmother pray. I wanted to learn how to pray like she did. I knew about the prayer meetings she had been part of, so I looked for one to visit. I remember walking into that musty old room where the ladies of the church were gathered. I was the only one under sixty. Forget that, I was the only one who still had all my teeth. These ladies looked at me funny and asked, "What are you here for?"

"I want to learn how to pray," I told them.

Each week, these anointed women of God, called The Mothers Board, taught me about prayer—that I could talk to God anytime; that prayer was about listening as well as talking; that prayer was sacrifice. They taught me how to set aside time for God and to seek Him with my whole heart. They let me know that God could not and would not ignore my pleas for help. These women loved me and spoke life into me like you'd never believe. They watered the seed of the Word that was in my life and taught me about a level of prayer I never knew existed. I became their son in the gospel.

In fact, these praying women so deeply engrained in me the sacrificial aspect of prayer that today, twice a month at our church, we hold a prayer meeting at 4 a.m., every second and fourth Tuesday. The Lord told me to call a prayer meeting, and I sensed Him saying, *This is going to be a sacrifice. Call it early.* We've been doing these meetings now for seven years, and I've never canceled a single one. At each one, about 500 to 600 people gather to pray—and God shows up!

But this prayer priority all started back in high school when I was just starting out in my chase. I learned to have conversations with God throughout my days, expressing my desperation, my desire to know and please Him, and my longing to walk and live the way He wanted me to live.

CHASING AFTER GOD IN HIS WORD

As I learned how to pray, I began to study the Word of God. One of the preachers at the church, a gentleman by the name of Edward Christian, came up to me one morning, pulled me close and invited me to this Bible study he led for young boys called the Timothy Club. Edward Christian was called to teach young boys the Word of God.

So in the same basement where I encountered Jesus for the first time, I met with other teenage boys every Thursday evening where Edward taught us to love the Word of God. He would cut up pieces of paper with verses on them and teach us how to search the Scriptures. Under Edward Christian, I learned how to study and read the Bible. He gave me my first study Bible and taught me how to highlight verses, how to memorize Scripture, how to relate God's Word to my life, and how to run references. Scripture tells us that God's Word matures us in our pursuit of Him. I experienced this firsthand. Just like newborn babies require milk to live and grow, we should crave the sincere milk of the Word so that, as Peter wrote to the exiles under religious persecution, we "may grow up in [our] salvation" (1 Peter 2:2).

Scripture tells us that God's Word matures us in our pursuit of Him.

Think back to the time Scripture came alive for you, and you realized its sustaining power. Now you have some idea of what was happening in my head and heart. If that hasn't happened for you yet, if Scripture is still just hard-to-understand words on a page, I implore you to find someone to join you in your chase, someone like an Edward Christian who loves the Word and thrives on seeing others discover the personal power and beauty of the Scriptures. You'll never be the same.

CHASING AFTER GOD IN COMMUNITY

The Babylonians trained young men of Judah to enter the service of King Nebuchadnezzar. For these young men, a nine-hundred-mile trip from the home they'd always known to an unfamiliar place and culture wasn't on their life agenda. By the time they made it to Babylon, a meal of the best cuts of meat and finest wine was prepared and offered to them.

> And the king appointed them a daily provision of the king's meat, and of the wine which he drank: so nourishing them three years, that at the end thereof they might stand before the king. (Dan. 1:5, KJV)

Now, you know this food probably looked, smelled, and tasted better than anything they were used to. But Daniel, Hananiah, Mishael, and Azariah knew they were different from the other young men around them. Scripture tells us that Daniel and his friends declined the royal food and wine and instead asked for a diet of vegetables and water, not wanting to defile themselves. And that's exactly why the enemy targeted them. Even when they were given Babylonian names—Belteshazzar

(Daniel), Shadrach, Meshach and Abednego, they didn't put up a fight because they already knew who they were in God. However, when it came to dishonoring their bodies, Daniel took a stand.

> Daniel then said to the guard whom the chief official had appointed over Daniel, Hananiah [Shadrach], Mishael [Meshach] and Azariah [Abednego], "Please test your servants for ten days: Give us nothing but vegetables to eat and water to drink. Then compare our appearance with that of the young men who eat the royal food, and treat your servants in accordance with what you see." So he agreed to this and tested them for ten days. (Dan. 1:11–14)

After ten days, the four Jewish men looked healthier and better nourished than any of the young men who had eaten the royal food—so *much* better that the guard allowed them to continue with their diet. And to these four young men, God gave knowledge and understanding of all kinds of literature and learning, including Daniel's ability to understand dreams and visions. By not bowing to the king's traditions and not conforming to the other men, Daniel and his friends stood out to the Babylonians and to God.

> As for these four children, God gave them knowledge and skill in all learning and wisdom: and Daniel had understanding in all visions and dreams. (Dan. 1:17, KJV)

My senior year of high school, I felt a little like Daniel and his friends as I repeatedly found myself with people and in situations that forced me to make choices and stand up for my faith. After encountering Jesus and getting involved in the Bible study, my circle of friends began to change. I had stopped partying, but some of my old friends still told me, "You'll be back. You'll be back to cursing. You'll be back to drinking. You'll be back to partying."

Like Daniel, though, I knew that God had called me out. I knew that I had been set apart. My mother and grandmother often told me the story of being at church one night when my mother, who was pregnant with me, felt like she was having a miscarriage. The presence of the Lord was so strong in the building that I began to kick in her womb.

She got up and went to my grandmother and told her, "Something's wrong. I think I might be losing the baby." My grandmother just looked at her and said, "Calm down, you're not having a miscarriage. God just sealed this child that's in your womb. He just literally put a call on this child." So many times, especially during those early years of being a Christian, I would come back to this story and remember, *No, I've been called out and set apart. I've been sealed for His glory.*

If there are people in your life who have taken the place God should hold, buckle up, because God is about to separate the wheat from the tares in your life.

In Paul's second letter to the church of Corinth, he told believers, "Therefore, come out from among unbelievers, and separate yourselves from them, says the Lord" (2 Cor. 6:17,

NLT). At this vulnerable time in my life, being so new in Christ, chasing after God meant that I had to be separated. If you're trying to hang on to people whose anointing no longer fits your life, if you're wrongly clinging to old friends just because you've known them all your life, you're about to be stripped. If there are people in your life who have taken the place God should hold, buckle up, because God is about to separate the wheat from the tares in your life.

Back then, I couldn't even be around people who were smoking because I had just quit. I remember one time feeling so desperate for a cigarette (I had no money to buy my own) that I walked around just trying to smell the smoke from other people's squares. When you're addicted to something, you'll find yourself doing some strange and crazy things! Desperate things! But when I encountered Jesus, I determined not to smoke anymore. Giving up cigarettes was a tremendous battle. But changing my circle of friends and surrounding myself with people who wanted to help, not hinder, my chase was key to conquering that addiction.

I experienced the same positive changes with my grades. Before I met Christ that March, my grades were terrible—I got into college on academic probation. But from March to graduation, my grades were better than they'd ever been. I was different. God was strengthening me.

In college, I refused to do the things that everyone else was doing and again, like Daniel and his band of brothers, began to see the hand of God on my life. I got into the right circle, with people who were like me—young, radical, and wanting to please God. They became the people I ate with and talked to for hours.

During that time, I met Mother Davis, a woman God just physically plopped into my life. I say that because there's just no other way to explain how the paths of young college students and someone like Mother Davis would cross. Some might call it serendipitous. I call it providential.

My friends were at a grocery store when they first met Mother Davis, a tall, slender but strong woman with smooth dark skin, and struck up a conversation with her. That day, she invited them to her home and they soon introduced me to her. We quickly learned that Mother Davis was a praying woman. She didn't have a television. She lived with very little, and she would say, "My house is dedicated to nothing but prayer." She always knew that God would send her people for the purpose of teaching them how to pray.

Mother Davis was downright weird, but that odd woman taught me so much. We built a special relationship with her. When we went to her house, we would have what she called shut-ins. We would lock up in her house all night, and she'd say, "We're going to pray an hour, and then we're going to read Scripture for an hour. We're going to pray an hour and then read an hour." Mother Davis taught me how to chase after God, how to pray for hours. Scripture tells us to "seek ye first the kingdom." She taught us how to seek God, how to be desperate for Him, and how to chase after Him.

In short, my surroundings—the places and people in my life—radically shifted. That's part of the chase—it's amazing!

So how do you chase after God and get to that place of desperation for Him? Three things: prayer—talking to and listening to God; the Word—studying what it says and what it means for your life; and community—surrounding yourself with people and places that bring true life.

CHAPTER 2

THE PEOPLE IN YOUR CHASE

ooking back at all the people God has brought into my life, I can see His handprints all over my past, present, and future. In many ways, God brought these people into my path to coach and run alongside me as together we chased after Him. It's really beautiful, isn't it?

If you choose wisely, the people you invite into the chase with you—your community—will help bring you closer to Jesus. That's what Edward Christian did in my life. Not only did he teach me to love and study the Word, he also mentored me. He bought me my first Bible, even gave me his phone number and said to call him when I needed someone to talk to or if I had questions about what I was studying. He made sure I could always talk to him about anything I was going through.

> *Out of the twenty boys who came to that basement every Thursday night for Bible study, fifteen of us became pastors.*

Even when I left for college in August, Edward kept up with me, called my dorm room, and sent me devotionals. He ran alongside me and, as he had been running much longer than me, even explained the chase to me. Edward showed me that living desperate for Jesus is a marathon, not a sprint. When I reflect on Edward's impact on my life, I think of Elijah and Elisha, Naomi and Ruth, and Paul and Timothy, and how the older leader taught and mentored the younger person, sometimes with their words, most often with their lives. Edward taught me with his life. He had encountered Christ at a young age and had gotten married as a virgin. He lived with sickle cell disease. I watched him endure sickness and go through a marriage separation. I saw how he responded when he was criticized. Throughout all those trials, his faith in God remained strong.

The Bible tells us to mark the perfect man (Ps. 37:37, KJV). Edward Christian was the one I marked in my chase. I wasn't the only one. Out of the twenty boys who came to that basement every Thursday night for Bible study, fifteen of us became pastors. Edward showed all of us what it looked like to live desperate for Jesus.

So Edward was the first leader to enter my life and teach me how to pursue a longing for Jesus. But while I was in college, I met Elder Willie James Campbell. I was home one summer and Edward looked at me in church and said, "You've outgrown this place. You need to go where you can be fed." So when I was nineteen, I went to Elder Campbell's church. Every time I came home from college, I was there. When I graduated and came back to Chicago, I became his right-hand man.

It was almost as if the Lord took me out of Edward's hands (he lost his battle with sickle cell while I was in college) and put me in the hands of Willie James Campbell, who became like a father figure to me. I was in my mid-twenties when Willie James got hold of me and taught me how to be a man, how to dress. He took me to top restaurants and taught me how to cut a steak with a fork and knife—basically he taught me everything my father and stepfather didn't. When I got married, he officiated at the wedding. When my mother passed, he preached her funeral.

He also taught me how to preach with power and authority, and how to fill the room with God's glory—to not stop until the presence of God filled the room. I saw him walk into some of the deadest places to preach, and just turn the building upside down. Sometimes he'd preach so hard he'd sweat. He'd always take out his handkerchief, wipe his face, and just keep on preaching. I still have some of those handkerchiefs. I would pick them up from the pulpit, almost like when Elisha picked up Elijah's cloak when he asked Elijah to give him a "double portion" of his spirit (2 Kings 2:9). I kept some of Elder Campbell's handkerchiefs and often asked God, *Let me have the same anointing to preach the way this man preaches.*

I was with him for nineteen years, which gave me unique access to him. I remember one time feeling so inadequate, like I would never be able to preach like he did, and I went to him.

"I don't know how God's going to use me," I said.

And he looked me in the eyes and said, "John, you find the vein that God wants to use you in, and you ask God to anoint that vein and you'll see a move of God."

It was the best advice—be comfortable with the way that God has given you to minister; but be anointed, and you'll see the hand of God move.

I also saw Willie James' struggles and learned from certain decisions he made. Because I walked close to him, I saw the good, the bad, and the ugly. That's part of coming alongside someone in their chase. As a mentor, you allow them to see everything: your virtues and your vices. As the mentee, you have the integrity and character not to exploit your leader's transparency. Getting next to someone who will be transparent with you will certainly help you in your chase. People who aren't afraid to be honest and open up their lives to others are secure in their identity as children of God. They have experienced unconditional love. Elder Willie James Campbell shared his gifts and his life to strengthen me in my chase and keep me desperate to know Jesus better.

Then there's Wilfredo "Choco" De Jesús who came alongside me and showed me what it looks like to chase after Jesus' heart for people. Choco recognized that while I may have been ready intellectually and theologically to lead a church, I was still lacking "a pastor's heart."

Now Choco and I are the same age, so my peer telling me I didn't have a pastor's heart didn't set too well. *Who is this guy telling me I need a heart for people?* But after I began serving at the local homeless shelter (at Choco's suggestion), I realized he was right. I realized that until I hurt for people like God does, I couldn't lead. No one wants to follow a leader whose heart doesn't bleed for his people. But man, it wasn't easy. I had to defeat the enemy of pride in a big way.

I still remember the day, ten-plus years ago, when Wilfredo said to me, "I see people following you now. Mark your sheep, so that when I plant you, we don't get our sheep mixed up." He told me to find my location, and I did. And he paid my first three months' rent. He bought my first sound system.

People who aren't afraid to be honest and open up their lives to others are secure in their identity as children of God.

And he took me to the bank to open up my first account. From that day on, at our church, New Life Covenant Southeast, every Sunday someone has walked the aisle to come to know the Lord.

Coming Alongside Others

Each of these influences in my life instilled in me the importance of running alongside others, both as a Timothy (being mentored) and as a Paul (mentoring others), in turn sharing what these leaders had taught me with those not yet in the chase or just starting it.

In college, my friends and I began having prayer meetings in our dorm rooms that eventually drew such a crowd we wound up going outside and praying on the football field. My desperation was so serious that my spiritual roots began to grow strong as I came alongside others in their chase. And because Edward Christian had taught me how to study the Word of God, I started leading Bible studies and even got the nickname "J the B," which stood for John the Baptist. When I walked across the campus, everyone would holler out, "J the B, J the B!" It was crazy, but that nickname drew people to me. They'd come to me when no one was around and begin to tell me their struggles. They needed someone to come alongside them.

My sophomore year, my roommate, Brad, came to me weeping. Brad was religious, but he didn't have a relationship with Jesus. He hadn't encountered Him. He was extremely sexually active, almost like a sexual addict, and one night Brad finally broke down, saying, "I don't want this kind of life."

When we as children of light live our lives in front of people, light overtakes darkness. I couldn't be in this dorm room with him, and my light not affect him.

From that night on, the light grew brighter with the two of us engaged with Jesus. Brad began to have honest conversations with me, both about his struggle and his desire to live right. He was watching and living around someone who maintained the chase. The same things that Edward did for me, I began to do for Brad. I pointed him to the Word and to prayer and accountability. He began coming to a Bible study I led and then to our football field prayer meetings. I walked with Brad throughout the year and tried to show him that right living begins with a desperate encounter with Jesus.

As I've led Bible studies, youth groups, youth conferences, a church on the south side of Chicago, even during my work as a juvenile probation officer, I've seen God move in people who live desperate lives—those with addictions, like my roommate; teens who are physically, emotionally, and sexually abused; young women selling their bodies and souls for money.

For ten years, I created and led the Inner City Youth Spring Break Conference in Chicago. Looking back, it was definitely my training ground for planting and leading a church.

At its height, we saw 15,000 kids. Each year, the conference was free, and each year I hustled to get money for these kids from sponsors, churches, philanthropists, grants, you name it. One year I was really struggling to raise the funds for it. I had a vision of me in an alley going through trash, and the Lord said to me, *This is where the church has put this generation, but I've assigned you to go to the ones the church has thrown out. My assignment to you is to minister to the forgotten, to give them the best, and to make sure they have an encounter so that they can begin their chase.*

I'm fifty-one years old now and have had numerous opportunities to come alongside others in their chase to know Jesus better. But by far, my favorite and most precious turn at mentoring came when I was twenty-six. I was sitting in church and saw this beautiful woman walk past me and put her offering in the plate. Eventually, I asked her name and later her phone number. Anna was new in the Lord when I met her. (That's a whole 'nother book on how to date and be a believer.) But I was careful not to mess up her chase and not to hinder her desperation for God. She and I dated for three years, and we've been married ever since.

Seeing people change and move away from destructive patterns, especially when God has used you in that transformation, will bring you closer to Him. There's something about coming alongside people and watching them go from leading desperate lives of addiction and aimlessness to becoming desperate for Jesus, desperate for deliverance, and desperate for walking in their purpose and their destiny that compels us to chase harder to know the depths of His power and love.

In This World

How do we live in this transformation and power even when life knocks us down flat? I'm encouraged that Jesus, who says He'll walk with us through our trials, is the One who tells us that we indeed will have trials. He knows what we will go through. In John's gospel, Jesus told His disciples, "I have told you these things, so that in me you may have peace. *In this world you will have trouble.* But take heart! I have overcome the world" (John 16:33, emphasis mine). And in Luke's gospel, Jesus told Simon Peter, "Simon, Simon, Satan has asked to sift all of you as wheat. But I have prayed for you, Simon, that your faith may not fail. And when you have turned back, strengthen your brothers" (Luke 22:31–32).

Yes, Jesus affirms what most of us already know and have experienced firsthand—this world is broken, and as believers we're not exempt from its shards. So how do we overcome our specific obstacles in life—the issues that threaten to take us out—to become and remain desperate for Him? Stay with me, friend, as we enter the next section of this book and look at six common obstacles that can hinder our desperation and learn how through prayer, the Word, and our community we can overcome our trials to find true life.

PART 2

OVERCOMING THE OBSTACLES

CHAPTER 3

THE HARDEST
OF HARD TIMES

B elieve me when I say I know firsthand what it feels like to take on the obstacle of hard times and how hard times in life can threaten to hinder your pursuit of Jesus.

Years ago, I was newly married, working a job I hated, and was really struggling with life when, boom! My mom was diagnosed with cancer. I felt like I'd just taken a hard kick to the stomach.

So my mom was sick, and we were reeling from the news of her diagnosis, wrestling with so many questions and concerns about her care. And in the midst of that, boom! I was laid off at my job. My wife and I were living in a tiny condo, my mother was sick, and suddenly I had no income. I applied for jobs, put feelers out for work, and applied for more jobs, but nothing. Nada. No income was coming in. And then, in just a matter of months, the worst possible thing happened: my mom passed away in July, just eight short months after her diagnosis.

I didn't think my life could get any harder.

My mom was gone, and I had no job or job prospects. Before she passed, my mom and I discussed that we would take in and adopt my fifteen-year-old sister because my stepfather couldn't handle raising her. So now I had a wife, a fifteen-year-old to raise, a deceased mother, and no job to support us. *Nothing* was coming in.

I can still remember the pressure and stress. My back was against the wall, and I wondered how all of this was going to work out. Those were *hard* times.

If you're alive and breathing, you might as well accept the fact that at some point in your life you'll face hard times, possibly the hardest of times when personal and work crises converge for the perfect storm.

The bills are piling up, and the tension at home is almost unbearable.

The test results come back positive, and the prognosis isn't good.

The kids are rebelling and making poor choices.

The parents are aging, and you're now the parent and caregiver.

The job search is full of dead ends.

Your grieving spouse has pulled away.

The relationship you trusted ends in betrayal.

There will come a time when you face a situation you can't handle on your own. The longer we live, the more we will come to those places where we don't know the answer or the next step.

And I can tell you from experience that when you get to those places, if you're not careful, you will maximize your struggle and minimize your God.

So hard times are coming. As followers of Jesus, we aren't exempt from the workings of a broken world. When you go through the valley, the key thing to remember is that God is right there in it with you. He isn't watching from a distance. He hasn't turned away His eyes. He is in the valley, in the chase, *with you.* Don't minimize God and His presence. Hold tight to His hand and to the truth that He's got you and will never let you go.

Psalm 37:25 says, "I was young and now I am old, yet I have never seen the righteous forsaken or their children begging bread." Ask God to come alongside you in your chase and as you walk beside Him, spend intentional time getting to know your Creator, your Savior, and your Father who will never forsake you. No matter how bleak the situation may look, He is with you. He is your provider. Matthew 6:26 says, "Look at the birds of the air; they do not sow or reap or store away in barns, and yet your heavenly Father feeds them. Are you not much more valuable than they?" I can't say it enough. God is with you. Don't ever doubt that.

I think of Pastor Farshid Fathi imprisoned in Iran for the "crime" of leading a network of underground house churches. Fathi converted from Islam to Christianity when he was seventeen and at age thirty-four was arrested and sentenced to six years in prison. The father of two has endured beatings and now shares a cell with criminals, receiving few family visits. He isn't permitted to sing hymns, and prison authorities took away his Bible. Pastor Fathi knows the hardest of times. But his letters from prison continue to reflect the faith of a man who truly

> *God is bigger than your hardest of hard times— whatever they are— and He is with you.*

understands that God is still with him. In December 2014, Fathi wrote: "Although the beauty of Christmas or the signs of Christmas cannot be found in this prison, with the ears of faith I can hear the everlasting and beautiful truth that: 'The virgin will conceive and give birth to a son, and they will call him Immanuel.'" Fathi signed the letter "Your captive brother who is free in Christ."[1]

Fathi has learned to hang tight to the truth and promise of Hebrews 13:5: "Never will I leave you; never will I forsake you." God is bigger than your hardest of hard times—whatever they are—and He is *with you*.

Deal or No Deal

For months, day in and day out, I would put on my nice clothes to go out and apply for yet another job. I'll never forget walking home after a day of job hunting and dead ends, feeling totally defeated. I put the key in the door, thinking, God, *you have to do something for me.* As I walked in the door, the phone rang. It was after 5 p.m., but I picked up the phone, and the voice on the line said, "We're looking for John Hannah. This is the juvenile court calling. Are you still interested in employment?"

More than a year before, I had applied for a job with the juvenile court for a probation officer position and had never heard so much as a word back. God came through in my desperate need.

Looking back now, I see two major reasons I made it through that wilderness:

1. God was with me; He never left me. At times, I felt Him carrying me.

2. I was adamant that I would not let my circumstances keep me from God. In spite of how I felt and what was going on, I made myself go to church and prayer meetings. I intentionally put myself in situations where I could hear from God, feel God, and be in His presence.

Hear me on this: If you allow your struggle to take over your pursuit of Jesus, hard times can take you out. Pretty soon, instead of chasing God, you're chasing employment. You're chasing comfort, a relationship. We tend to chase after whatever we believe will take away the pain and eliminate or minimize the struggle.

In Exodus 14, as the Israelites reached the Red Sea, fearing for their lives, Moses said to the people, "Do not be afraid. Stand firm and you will see the deliverance the LORD will bring you today" (Ex. 14:13). In other words, you can't make anything happen for yourself, people. You never could. Only God can fight for you. Only God will give you what you need. There are no substitutes.

I had been waiting and waiting for something, anything, to happen in my life. But while I was standing still, awaiting deliverance—my back up against the wall tighter than ever—I was determined not to compromise who I was, not to compromise my faith. Then I saw God literally step in. He provided the seemingly impossible help exactly when I needed it.

Word Up

When hard times hit, we have to learn to lean into God's Word, which means we have to know His Word. Scriptures such as:

The LORD is my light and my salvation—whom shall I fear? The LORD is the stronghold of my life—of whom shall I be afraid? (Ps. 27:1)

For I am the LORD your God who takes hold of your right hand and says to you, "Do not fear; I will help you." (Isa. 41:13)

"I have told you these things, so that in me you may have peace. In this world you will have trouble. But take heart! I have overcome the world." (John 16:33)

Do not be anxious about anything, but in every situation, by prayer and petition, with thanksgiving, present your requests to God. And the peace of God, which transcends all understanding, will guard your hearts and your minds in Christ Jesus. (Phil. 4:6–7)

My God shall supply all your needs according to his riches in glory. (Phil. 4:19, KJV)

Cast all your anxiety on him because he cares for you. (1 Peter 5:7)

Blessed is the one who perseveres under trial because, having stood the test, that person will receive the crown of life that the Lord has promised to those who love him. (James 1:12)

These words were like gold to me. I've memorized these powerful Scriptures, and they've been part of an ongoing conversation with God. Many times, I read the Word to remind myself of who God is, what He has promised, and who I am in His sight. I speak the truth over myself and back to Him, saying things like, *God, I'm yours. I'm your child. You are the good shepherd. You've said you'll leave the ninety-nine to come and find the one.* I remind myself of the truth of God's Word and what it says about the depths of His love and provision for us, especially in hard times. And I remind myself, as the Scripture reminds me, that hard times do not last forever. This is just a season, a challenging season, yes, but it isn't permanent.

When hard times hit, we have to learn to lean into God's Word, which means we have to know His Word.

The Word of God is powerful and keeps us focused on truth in the middle of the drought. But at the same time, you need to know your next move.

I think about Elijah, on the run from Jezebel, when he ended up at a well in the middle of a drought and the well ran dry—no more water. What do most of us tend to do when faced with a drought, when the well runs dry? We just stay where we are, instead of seeking God for our next move. Why do we keep looking into an empty well, in hopes of water suddenly appearing? What's your next move?

Truthfully, until you're desperate, you won't know what to do next—until you press into that desperation for God. When you press in, when you continue to chase after God, He gives you your next move. He answers "What next?"—even if that next move is just standing still or walking.

In 1 Kings 17, God told Elijah, "Okay, the well is dry. Now leave this well. Go to a brook in the Kerith Ravine and drink from the brook and the ravens will feed you there." What if Elijah had just stayed at the dry well? Without food and without water, he would've died. But Elijah was still sensitive to God's Spirit; Elijah was still pressing in. And because he listened, he heard God's instruction.

When hard times come, you'll either see God meet the need right there on the spot, or in standing still and pressing into that desperation for God, He'll give you instructions on how to proceed. He'll give you a next move. However it shakes out, God *will* manifest Himself in that dry place.

God had sent ravens to feed the people in the land where Elijah lived. God did a supernatural thing. When the well ran dry where Elijah was hiding, the ravens kept coming. But he couldn't survive without water.

When we think of God's provision, we often just consider that thing we're most in need of—a new job, healing of the sick, the desire of our heart—but we also need to see God's provision in His Word, in Scripture.

When Hard Times Last

I realize you might be saying, "Well, John Hannah, that's all fine and good, but you don't know how long I've been in this drought. You don't know the trouble I've seen." And you'd be right. I've known many people who have experienced much longer and harder seasons than what I've experienced. I've known people who have struggled for years with debilitating illness, with little to no chance of survival. They've been in a hard place for so long they can't even remember what it looks like not to be there, what it feels like to be free.

I think about Job and how he took hit after hit: first his animals, then his home, and then all of his children. His wife was ready to check out. When she told Job, "Curse God and die," Job said something so powerful. He told her (Job 2:10), "Shall we accept good from God, and not trouble?" He had no idea why all these terrible things were happening in his life, but instead of reacting with *Why me? What have I done to deserve this?* Job said, "Though he slay me, yet will I hope in him" (Job 13:15). He stayed his course with God, choosing to trust Him, even in his darkest days, in his hardest of hard times.

The real question is: How did Job manage to stay faithful through so much adversity and suffering? Books have been written on that question. For me, the answer is simple. Job acknowledged God as sovereign and continued to trust in His sovereignty. We live in a broken, sinful world. Life is going to come at you and hit you. At times, it's going to blindside you with one blow after another. Your pursuit of God is the place where you'll find comfort, where you'll get wisdom. In your pursuit, in your desperation for Him, you'll discover direction. In your desperation, you come to know, firsthand, that He is God and that He is up to something.

Scripture tells us the story of Ruth's mother-in-law, Naomi. The book of Ruth begins with a famine in the land—hard times all around. Then Naomi's husband died. She became a widow. Then her sons died. Her entire support system was gone. With no one to support her and famine all around, Naomi decided to return to her hometown. She had heard that the Lord was providing food for His people in Bethlehem. Her widowed daughter-in-law, Ruth, begged to go with her. It took all of these trying times to get Ruth into the company of Boaz, whom Ruth eventually married. As a result, she ended up being the great-great-grandmother of King David. She is one of two women listed in the lineage of Jesus (Matt. 1:1–16).

Take note how Naomi pursued God during her most difficult days, during her drought. She moved from that place of death and famine toward a place where God was at work. She kept pursuing Him to see what He was up to and how she and Ruth might be part of the story He was writing. She believed in His provision.

Community: Who's Got Your Back?

When hard times hit, the worst thing you can do is surround yourself with people who are negative and cynical, people who are going to speak crazy into your life. Words have a powerful impact, for good or for bad—especially in trying times.

I'll take that even further: When you hit a hard season in your life, not only do you need positive truth-tellers and wisdom-speakers in your life, you also need to surround yourself with people who do more than talk. You need doers around you—people who will carry you when your strength gives out.

In Luke 5, Jesus was teaching in a house, and the place was packed out. Knowing that Jesus was there, and that He could heal people (He had recently healed a leper), a group of friends came up with a risky plan. Desperate to get their paralyzed friend in front of Jesus, the friends carried the man up to the roof of the house, actually broke through the roof, and lowered their friend down on his mat in front of Jesus. These guys weren't taking no for an answer. They would not give up until they found a way to get their friend to Jesus.

When you're at your lowest, surround yourself with people of faith. The Bible says that when Jesus saw the faith of this man's friends—not necessarily the man lying there on the bed—He healed him: "When Jesus saw *their* faith, he said, 'Friend, your sins are forgiven'" (Luke 5:20, emphasis mine).

Sometimes, when hard times hit, your faith can waver. You're in a weak spot, emotionally, physically, and spiritually. Having faithful people around you in hard times—people who can carry you to Jesus—is vital. God hears the prayers of others lifting you up. Like the friends of the paralytic, He sees *their* faith and blesses *you*. When you can't pray, surround yourself with prayer warriors.

> *When hard times hit, the worst thing you can do is surround yourself with people who are negative and cynical, people who are going to speak crazy into your life.*

When you can't stand, surround yourself with people who'll stand for you and with you.

I remember times when I couldn't pray, when I simply didn't have the words. During those trying times, I made it a priority to get around people who could and would pray for me. To get through hard times, immerse yourself in prayer, the Word, and your community—people who will bring you to the Father.

From the beginning of my pursuit, as I've matured in my faith, my circle of community has changed. Now, when life hits me hard, those who would have handed me a cigarette, those who would have passed me a joint, are not in my circle anymore. They're no longer around to make a bad situation even worse. Now when I hit a wall, I'm surrounded with people who come alongside me, pray for me, strengthen me, and carry me.

When my mom died, I was devastated. We were very close. She was a rock in my life, and I talked with her every day. I remember picking up the phone to call her and thinking, *Oh, I can't call her now.* I went through major depression. My whole world seemed off its course, off the axis somehow. By God's grace, I stayed in pursuit. I didn't revert back to old habits or run to old friends because my circle had changed.

I remember one night waking up from a restless sleep, and I was just torn up. The grief was overwhelming, so I called my elder, Pastor Willie James Campbell, in the middle of the night and told him, "Pastor, I'm losing it."

He began to speak life to me. "You're not going to lose it; you're going to be fine," he said. "This is what is called grief, and you're going to get through this hard time. You will see, hear, or sense the hand of God." The only way I survived that season—one of the most difficult things I've ever faced—was through people in my life who spoke truth, who spoke life, who prayed for me, and refused to let me go.

My wife is that way. Her presence alone speaks volumes. Anna doesn't force words on me. She's not one to spend a lot of time trying to talk me out of discouragement. But she prays for me. I've awakened to see her in prayer for me and have felt her hand on me as she prayed. When I'm struggling or feeling down, she gives me space to seek God and to be alone with Him. She battles hard for me in silence.

So let that be a word, friend: Whether you've hit a hard time yet or not, surround yourself with the kind of people who will battle for you, people who will carry you, people who—like you— are desperate to get to Jesus.

The Cave

When it comes to material things, the means to survive, God will send someone or something to pull you out of where you are. Either that, or He'll reorder your steps to a new place.

But when it comes to great loss and emotional devastation, even the godly people you surround yourself with may not be able to relieve your pain or help you work through your grief. You may need some counseling to help you get the emotional and spiritual healing you need.

Writer Daphne Merkin once described depression as a "thick black paste covering one's life."[2] That seems accurate. I look back on what I went through with the loss of my mother, and I know I should've gone to counseling to work through my grief. I just couldn't shake it. Every Mother's Day, I had a date with depression. I didn't go to church because I didn't want to celebrate mothers when I was still grieving mine. That date with depression lasted about seven years—seven years! That's too long.

By giving me the opportunity to minister at a Mother's Day banquet, of all things, God forced me out of that dark place. Using humor and laughter to emcee that event, I was able to begin the healing process. If I had gotten the right professional help to begin with, I would've emerged from that pit sooner.

It's almost impossible to chase after God when you're in a cave. So in talking about life's troubles and how they hinder us from chasing after God, we need to talk about the cave we tend to duck into and sometimes dwell in when we're struggling. When you get so buried under by the weight of your situation, it's easy to wind up there. In the cave, we can't do much. We can barely move. It's dark, difficult to see, with no view of what's in front of us. In the cave, the light eludes us. We aren't able to stay focused on our pursuit of God.

> *When you find yourself looking for a cave to retreat into during your hard times, it's time to listen to the voice of God asking, "What are you doing here?"*

Elijah knew that cave well. Going back to his story, when he was on the run from Queen Jezebel who was clearly out to kill him (1 Kings 19)—Elijah went through major depression. He was running for his life. He had left his servant in Beersheba, so he was all alone, with no one around to speak wisdom to him. He ended up under a tree, not eating, wallowing in his misery. But God woke him up and commanded an angel to feed him. God provided strength for Elijah's journey.

Elijah grew stronger but not whole. When he wound up in a cave for the night, Scripture tells us that God said to him, "What are you doing here, Elijah" (1 Kings 19:9)? God forced Elijah to examine and articulate what he was doing, and then told him to come out of the cave and go to the mountain "in the presence of the LORD" where He will pass by (1 Kings 19:11). There, God revealed Himself in a soft whisper, an expression that resonated loudly with Elijah. Out of the cave, God revealed Himself in Elijah's life and gave him instructions on what to do next.

When you find yourself looking for a cave to retreat into during your hard times, it's time to listen to the voice of God asking, *What are you doing here?*

In Due Season

Life brings us hard seasons. King Solomon makes this clear in the famous passage of Ecclesiastes 3:1–8, (books, poems, songs, even movie lines have found their inspiration from these eight beautiful verses):

There is a time for everything,
and a season for every activity under the heavens:
a time to be born and a time to die,
a time to plant and a time to uproot,
a time to kill and a time to heal,
a time to tear down and a time to build,
a time to weep and a time to laugh,
a time to mourn and a time to dance
a time to scatter stones and a time to gather them,
a time to embrace and a time to refrain from embracing,

a time to search and a time to give up,
a time to keep and a time to throw away,
a time to tear and a time to mend,
a time to be silent and a time to speak,
a time to love and a time to hate,
a time for war and a time for peace.

Everything happens in a season. In other words, it won't always be like this. But sometimes, when seasons end, we do the worst thing possible: We do our best to stretch them out. It's all we've known for so long that we keep hanging on, trying to keep things the way they were. We're often in denial about the season we're in. It's over, but we haven't moved on. We try to change it, but fail to see that what's done is done, that for everything there is a *season*. It's over. Yes, we're going to grieve. Yes, it will be hard. But there comes a time to let the season come to an end, to let it be over.

Job's tragic story made this oh so clear. In chapter 1, at the beginning of the book of Job, he said, "The LORD gave, and the LORD has taken away: may the name of the LORD be praised" (Job 1:21). Then at the end of the book, Job reinforced his trust in God's sovereignty: "[God] knows the way that I take; when he has tested me, I will come forth as gold" (Job 23:10). Job, who lost everything, knew that even his darkest season would eventually pass.

Throughout my season of hard times, I stayed faithful to pray (or asked others to pray for me); I read the Word and surrounded myself with a community of people who loved God and loved me. I did what I knew to do and kept getting up in the morning. My prayer is that you'll do the same during your hard times and that when the season is over, you'll let it be over and move forward.

The End of You Is The
Beginning of Desperation

Without the Word, without prayer, and in the absence of uplifting people, hard times will take their toll on you and on your chase. When we're not seeking the Lord, when there's nothing good surrounding us, when we're not reading the Word, when we can't feel the Spirit of God moving in our lives, we will turn inward. We will turn to ourselves. And when that happens—when we take matters into our own hands—the hard season we're in only gets harder.

That was the case with King Saul, the first king over Israel. There he was, in 1 Samuel 31, wounded on a battlefield, asking an armor-bearer to stab him and end his life. When the armor-bearer wouldn't do it, what did Saul do? He took his own sword and fell on it. He took matters into his own hands, not seeking God's wisdom, and in the end, he couldn't deal with the aftermath of his choices.

Here's something the world won't tell you: Don't trust yourself, especially in hard times, because you're not trustworthy. You're made of human flesh and if you put yourself in charge of your destiny, the way becomes even more dangerous (more on the desires of the flesh in chapter 8). You've got to get to the end of you.

The good news is this: At the end of you is the beginning of desperation. We can only become desperate for Jesus when our human desires are at their weakest. When we're hopeless. So if, in that moment, we turn to ourselves, we're certainly not desperate for Jesus. Being desperate for Him means trusting Him and only Him, believing that He will take you out of this season you're in right now.

And He *will* get you out.

The gospels record an account of Jesus and the disciples on a boat when a huge storm rose up on the Sea of Galilee. The disciples went into panic mode. Just imagine them being whipped all around that boat by wind and rain and the sea! They literally feared for their lives. Thank God they didn't just jump overboard. I'm pretty sure that thought came up at some point. What did they do? They ran straight to Jesus who was in the bottom of the boat sleeping. They woke Him up saying, "Don't you care that we're about to die?"

Now, that's desperation, waking up their sleeping leader. That's also prayer. Think about it. They didn't huddle up trying to figure out a game plan or scream life-saving measures to each other. Instead, they went straight to the source of their rescue. They knew their Lord was sleeping. They knew He would help them, and so they ran, fearing for their lives, to Jesus. That's *prayer.*

When life hits you hard, when the storm rises up, tossing you to and fro, don't trust yourself or take matters into your own hands. Not when you have the Savior of the world on your side. Go to Him. Go to Jesus. Ask Him to speak the Word into your situation. Ask Him for help in the storm . . . because He will help. He knows your seasons, He's in the boat *with you,* and He will help.

A Desperate Prayer:

Lord, I pray that You never allow my needs to outweigh my hunger and thirst for You. Just as You led the prophet Elijah to the brook in a time of drought and then led him to the widow when the brook dried up, I pray that You will lead me. I believe Your Word's promises that all of my

needs will be met according to Your riches in glory. So I
thank You in advance that You have proven Yourself to be
faithful in the hardest of hard times.

CHAPTER 4

THE STRIFE OF RELATIONSHIPS

When Thomas Edison debuted his idea for a new invention called the light bulb, I wonder if he anticipated all of the naysayers who would come out of the woodwork to doubt him, to disparage his ideas and his work.

Henry Morton, president of the Stevens Institute of Technology, publicly said, "Everyone acquainted with the subject will recognize it as a conspicuous failure."[1]

The British Parliamentary Committee arrogantly referred to it as ". . . good enough for our transatlantic friends . . . but unworthy of the attention of practical or scientific men."[2]

An 1879 newspaper article reported, "The truth is that Mr. Edison, although very successful in discovering improvements in subjects in which he was practically engaged, lacks the knowledge and training, which have persuaded the greatest chemists in the world of the inadaptability of electricity for general lighting purposes."[3]

Some of the harshest words of Edison's contemporaries were recorded in the *Kalamazoo Gazette* in 1879: "Very few of the many investigators who had studied the subject of electric lighting believed that the experiments [by Edison] would prove important. . . . Not having been properly educated in early life, he was ignorant, so they said, of the properties of matter."[4]

Few people believed in Edison and his dream of bringing incandescent light to the world. Most criticized him. Sometimes the biggest speed bumps in our lives are people who don't believe in us and what we value.

What if those naysayers are your family—your own flesh and blood? How do you deal with that? How do you continue your chase for true life when the people closest to you don't understand you or your pursuit of God? To them, you're a little off, just a skosh out of touch with reality, maybe "ignorant," like Edison's critics described him.

> *Sometimes even the people closest to us—husband, wife, children, siblings, parents, close friends—don't understand us and what God is doing in our lives.*

Joseph (yes, *that* Joseph with the coat of many colors) found himself surrounded by family who didn't believe in him. God had spoken to him in two dreams, and unfortunately he shared his dreams with his brothers and father. They didn't "get" it. They didn't have dreams. They didn't have passion. Even worse, the Bible says that when Joseph told them about his dreams, his brothers hated him, questioned the validity of his dreams ("So you think you will be our king, do you? Do you actually think you will reign over us?"), and they cursed him.

You want to talk about family that doesn't "get" you, look no further than David. In 1 Samuel 17, David set out to take food to his brothers in the field, and Goliath stepped out. When David dared to inquire about Goliath, David's older brother, Eliab, turned around and rebuked him, basically saying, "I know your heart."

> When Eliab, David's oldest brother, heard him speaking with the men, he burned with anger at him and asked, "Why have you come down here? And with whom did you leave those few sheep in the wilderness? I know how conceited you are and how wicked your heart is; you came down only to watch the battle." (1 Sam. 17:28)

Eliab pretty much belittled his youngest brother in front of the other men who were standing there.

Sometimes even the people closest to us—husband, wife, children, siblings, parents, close friends—don't understand us and what God is doing in our lives. What really hurts is that most of the time, they won't even *try* to understand it.

Even Jesus experienced this speed bump. The Feast of Booths was approaching and Jesus' brothers wanted Him to reveal Himself. They said to Him:

> "Leave here and go into Judea, so that Your disciples also may see Your works which You are doing. For no one does anything in secret when he himself seeks to be known publicly. *If* you do these things, show

Yourself to the world." For not even His brothers were believing in Him. (John 7:3–5, NASB, emphasis mine)

Jesus' brothers (James, Joses, Simon, and Judas—no, not *that* Judas) had grown up with Jesus and had seen Him teach at the temple. They would've known about some of His miracles (the wedding at Cana, feeding the five thousand, etc.). Yet His own flesh and blood didn't believe in Him. Friend, don't ever think you're alone in your feelings of being misunderstood. Jesus knows firsthand what it's like to have the people closest to you doubt you.

Even when we know deep down that our family doesn't support us, we often still look to them to validate us and to appreciate our chase for God and its significance in our lives. We want to know they believe in us. We need it. Sometimes, though, we have to resolve that it's simply not going to happen. My biological father couldn't teach me to be a man of God. My stepfather couldn't teach me. It was tough. I had to get to a place where I could accept that they weren't going to be there for me in that way. They're not it. And that's difficult because we expect and want our parents to be it, to understand, to "get" us.

So sometimes in this chase, God replaces your family, which can be very difficult to understand and accept. In my own life, He replaced my father and stepfather—those who couldn't be there for me or understand who I was becoming—and then supported me with people like my grandmother, my mother, Edward Christian, Willie James Campbell, Mother Davis, Wilfredo De Jesús, and others who could and would speak truth into my life.

Believe me, we can put too much energy into trying to win family members' approval, which ultimately distracts us from our chase. We try to get them to understand, try to persuade them to see things the way we see them—to no avail. I've seen people allow their family members, even their spouses, to kill the passion they have for God—passion given to them by God. How do we weather the naysayers in our lives? Check out how Jesus responded to His unbelieving brothers.

Did He lash out against them? No, and He didn't try to convince them that He was the Son of God, either. He simply stated His purpose: "My time is not yet here; for you any time will do. The world cannot hate you, but it hates me because I testify that its works are evil. You go to the festival. I am not going up to this festival, because my time has not yet fully come" (John 7:6–8).

David didn't address his brother. Instead of letting that speed bump knock him off course, he continued on with his inquiry about Goliath, until Saul heard that the young boy David was willing to fight the Philistine giant—and I'm guessing you know the rest of the story. David took five smooth stones and with a simple slingshot took Goliath out!

Joseph didn't let his brothers downplay or kill his dream. He continued to believe in the vision God had given Him and continued to trust Him during the hardest of hard times.

Let's look at a later chapter in David's life. At that time, he was king of Israel, and he went to get the ark of the covenant and bring it back to his city (2 Sam. 6). If you really study this story, you can almost feel how passionate David was about his mission of bringing the glory of God home. Saul, his predecessor, never went after the ark. David was so excited when he finally brought the ark into the city that the Bible says he danced before the Lord with all his might and blessed God with words, dance, and sacrifices. And then he turned around and blessed the people.

But when David came home to bless his house, his wife, Michal, met him at the door and she was livid. She let him have it in no uncertain terms: "How the king of Israel has distinguished himself today," she spit, clearly speaking with contempt for what he had done, "going around half-naked in full view of the slave girls of his servants as any vulgar fellow would" (2 Sam. 6:20)! In other words, *David, you're such an embarrassment . . . to yourself, to me, and to your office.* Michal, daughter of Saul, didn't understand David's pursuit of God.

Look at David's response to her. He didn't respond in anger. He just spoke plainly, saying, "It was before the LORD, who chose me rather than your father or anyone from his house when he appointed me ruler over the LORD's people Israel—I will celebrate before the LORD. I will become even more undignified than this, and I will be humiliated in my own eyes" (vv. 21–22). What a radical thing to say! *You think this is embarrassing, Michal, just wait . . . there is nothing I won't do in worship of the Lord.* Verse 23 says Michal never had children because God punished her for speaking against David's unrestrained worship. But David maintained his praise, his persistence, and his desperation for God.

So it comes down to this: If your family doesn't understand what God is doing in your life, and why you're chasing after Him, then they haven't had the encounter with Him that you've had.

But there is hope. I thank God He is a God of reconciliation and restoration. I'm always encouraged when I read that even though David's brothers rebuked him, when push came to shove for David, his brothers showed up for him. In a cold, dark, and dank cave where David had run to, hiding out from Saul, his brothers got to him first and came alongside him. We can have hope that, eventually, our family will come around.

In my family, I'm the oldest brother, and there was a time when one of my younger brothers didn't care for me. I hadn't done anything to him, but he didn't appreciate my calling or the way I lived my life. Truthfully, he was not living for the Lord. He was messed up, a drug dealer. I didn't let his disapproval stop me from going after God or infect my heart against God. I didn't allow him—or our estranged relationship—to distract me from what God had for me. And when I became a pastor, I began to call out his name in prayer, and I asked God to save my brother. What could've been a stumbling block became a matter of prayer, and today my brother is saved and is a member of my church.

I've learned that our assignment is not to put our hands on our family and try to change their hearts. That's up to God.

I've learned that our assignment is not to put our hands on our family and try to change their hearts. That's up to God. We have to let them be who they are. When David's brother spoke against him, David didn't address it. When Jesus' brothers basically said, "We don't believe in you," He stayed focused and kept moving, knowing His mission.

In Philippians 3:14 (KJV), Paul tells us to "press toward the mark for the prize of the high calling of God." I like the encouragement *The Message* offers us in this passage:

> I've got my eye on the goal, where God is beckoning us onward—to Jesus. I'm off and running, and I'm not turning back. So let's keep focused on that goal, those

of us who want everything God has for us. If any of you have something else in mind, something less than total commitment, God will clear your blurred vision— you'll see it yet! Now that we're on the right track, let's stay on it. (Phil. 3:14–15, *The Message*)

Is it time to make God your mark and stay in pursuit of Him? Be desperate for *Him*—not validation from your family, friends or others around you. I get that the strife of relationships is tough. It can take you out! To overcome it, we have to follow the lead of Jesus, David, and Joseph and stay focused on the goal of true life.

What You Hear and What You See

So we've established that you will always have people in your life who don't "get" what you're about, people who will distract you from the goal. How do you identify these people? It's not too difficult. Listen to their words and watch their spirit.

Words are powerful. Even a few of them can speak volumes about the state of a person's heart. Words can be subtle and cutting all at once. Then there's actions or behavior. Watch what someone does and what motivates that person to do what they do. In both someone's words and especially their actions, we see their spirit. Scripture gives us specific instruction about what a person's tongue (words) and actions say about them:

Death and life are in the power of the tongue, and those who love it will eat its fruits. (Prov. 18:21, ESV)

Every good tree bears good fruit, but a bad tree bears bad fruit. A good tree cannot bear bad fruit, and a bad tree cannot bear good fruit. (Matt. 7:17–18).

In Genesis, we read about the first murder ever recorded in history. The sons of Adam and Eve quickly reaped the curse of a fallen world. Cain was envious of his brother Abel. Had Abel paid attention to his brother's spirit—his words and his actions—he never would have ventured out to the fields and into the path of his murderous brother.

When the words and actions of those around you negatively impact you, remember your priorities. Stay calm and look at the big picture. Just as it was for David and for Joseph, much bigger things await you. The kingdom of God is bigger than the validation and praise of others. Ask yourself, *Which is more important, your friendship with someone or God's favor? Your acceptance by others or God's acceptance of you?* Know the kind of people around you by the words they speak and the spirit revealed in their actions. Remember that those people are only pebbles on your path. If you can recognize them as such, the distraction factor begins to fade.

When you're desperate for Jesus, He is your mark. Nothing less.

Knowing that, Satan will use whatever or whomever he can to get you off course. He is no respecter of persons. He will even use your children. And when your children come after you, you have to give them to God. You have no choice.

Jesus said that He came, not to bring peace, but to bring a sword, to divide father from son and mother from daughter:

"Anyone who loves their father or mother more than me is not worthy of me; anyone who loves their son or daughter more than me is not worthy of me. Whoever does not take up their cross and follow after me is not worthy of me. Whoever finds their life will lose it, and whoever loses their life for my sake will find it." (Matt. 10:37–39)

That is the price tag that comes with a life of chasing after Jesus.

Keep Moving, No Matter What

Following Jesus doesn't mean you'll be perfect. Following Him, or chasing after Him, just means that you stay in the chase. No matter what.

If you think about it, Abraham—the father of all who believe (Rom. 4:16) and the survivor of multiple tests (from picking up and leaving his home in Ur to his willingness to sacrifice his son, Isaac)—had some serious hiccups in his pursuit of God.

That's why God told Abraham in Genesis 12, "Get out of your father's house. Get out from around your people. Step out, and then you'll begin to see the blessings of the LORD on your life." At the age of seventy-five, God told this man who knew nothing else but his father's house to leave and to move on. Leave everything, leave everybody, and step out into La La Land . . . and then you'll see the blessings of the Lord.

Now I'm not sure if seventy-five years old back then was like seventy-five now, but we can't overlook the importance of that move. Decades later, then elderly Abraham would make his servant, Eliezer, promise him that he wouldn't let Isaac go back to Abraham's home country of Ur. Think about that: As hard as a move like that must have been for Abraham, he knew it was ultimately for his good to leave and he didn't want Isaac to fall into his dad's former complacency.

Before God called him out, Abram (God later changed his name to Abraham) was raised in a godless house with a godless religion. But Abram had dissenting views—he believed there was another creator besides the sun—and often wound up arguing with those around him. When God called Abram out of Ur, He called him to leave that place of temptation and strife. He knew that Abram would never find the true life He had for him in the house of his father. Living in pursuit of God while being surrounding by negativity is crazy difficult. Thriving and pressing on to the greater goal while being around complacent people who don't understand you or your beliefs can feel almost impossible. That's why our surroundings are so important.

Being surrounded by people who unabashedly encourage us to press on to the mark is essential.

In 1996 while training for the 2002 Winter Olympics in Salt Lake City, U.S. skier Picabo Street tore a crucial ligament in her left knee. At thirty years old (she first joined the U.S. ski team, at age seventeen), Street made it to the Olympics, having gone through extensive and often painful rehabilitation. Was the work and pain worth it? In an interview with *The New York Times*, Street said, "The last four years for me have been about that one moment coming into the finish when I heard the Americans roar and saw kids' faces painted red, white, and blue."[5]

Being surrounded by people who unabashedly encourage us to press on to the mark is essential. We all need those encouraging words. We need those people who will cheer for us, who will pray for us and with their words, and by their actions consistently remind us to get up, even when we're wounded, and keep moving. Let me be clear here. If you have a spouse who doesn't believe in God, I'm not suggesting you leave or move on from your marriage. However, you do need to surround yourself with people who will encourage and run alongside you in your chase. And you do need to continue to pray and study the Word, resolving to pray for your spouse and keep moving toward the mark.

The Promise Is Greater

Now you might remember that God had promised Abraham he would one day be the father of a great nation. But every time the still childless Abraham pondered his age, he doubted the promise. Finally, when Abraham was eighty-five and still with no offspring, Sarah decided to take matters into her own hands to start a family and sent her servant, Hagar, to sleep with Abraham. And he did. Don't miss that! He could have refused and waited on God. When Abraham was eighty-six, Hagar had Ishmael, Abraham's firstborn (Gen. 16). Then Genesis 17:1 says that Abraham was ninety-nine years old. He was eighty-six in chapter 16 and a chapter later he is ninety-nine?

Thirteen years had passed. Thirteen years with no communication from God. All Abraham could do was watch his mistake grow and listen to God's silence. Nothing. Not a word.

More than a decade later, the Lord reappeared to Abraham and reintroduced Himself saying, "I am God Almighty; walk before me faithfully and be blameless" (Gen. 17:1). In other words, "Get up, son, let's go."

I wonder if Abraham was so ashamed that he didn't even try to talk to God during those thirteen years. The Bible says there were no more children by Hagar, so essentially, that was that. Abraham was standing still, focused on his mistake. Some people would try to leave, to go back to where they came from, but he didn't go back to his father's people. Instead, he stood still and waited on God for thirteen years. And then, in Genesis 17:16, God said, "I will. I will. I will." I *will* bless Sarah, now ninety years old, with a child. At age one hundred, Abraham, you *will* bear a son with her. She *will* be the mother of nations, and kings *will* come from your lineage.

So even though Abraham sinned with Hagar, God brought the promise back to him and told him, "Abraham, you waited on me thirteen years. Because you didn't allow this situation to overtake you, I'm going to give My promise to you in one year. You didn't go backwards. You didn't go back to your father's people. You didn't continue with Hagar. You didn't let people pull you down. You stood still and waited on me. Now get up and walk before Me."

Sometimes standing still and waiting on God in our pursuit after we've allowed people to hinder our chase, gives God room to work in our lives, to come and remind us of who He is and what He will do. Sometimes in our standing still and waiting on God, we are also chasing Him. That's definitely a paradox—but a profound one that we see throughout Scripture.

As sons of Abraham, we will make mistakes. Life is full of poor choices and the consequences of those choices. Do we learn from those mistakes, or do we keep birthing sin after sin, to the point that we give up on God's promise of true life?

I want you to get this: Your mistakes cannot ever outweigh God's love for you and your desperation for Him. If you've given into the words or the spirits of people, stand still and wait because the chase *will* continue. Maintain your desperation. Yes, there will always be consequences for our mistakes, but the promise of true life is so much greater.

A Desperate Prayer

Father, I thank You that regardless of the strife in various relationships, You have been a friend who sticks closer than a brother. I pray that You would give me the ability to stand still and know that all things are going to work together for my good. So I commit all my relationships to You and ask that You will keep my heart pure from all evil against anyone.

CHAPTER 5

THE BLOW OF BETRAYAL

n this pursuit of Christ, one of the most difficult obstacles you'll face, especially when it comes to relationships, is betrayal. Mark my word. You are going to be betrayed.

Someone you trust will turn on you. And at the point of impact, it will hurt beyond your ability to understand. The great American playwright Steven Dietz sheds light on the heart-wrenching pain of betrayal: "One should rather die than be betrayed. There is no deceit in death. It delivers precisely what it has promised. Betrayal, though . . . betrayal is the willful slaughter of hope."[1]

Chances are you've experienced that staggering blunt-force trauma to the gut—the sucker-punch that leaves you reeling. Some of you have felt that blow of betrayal repeatedly throughout your life to the point where now there's not much trust left in you.

The worst part of betrayal? The fact that you can only be truly betrayed by someone you're close to, someone you've let into your heart and your life. Someone you've opened the door to and invited into your intimate circle. Someone in your family. One of your closest friends. People outside your circle of trust can't betray you. That devastating role is reserved for insiders, those in whom you've placed great confidence and trust.

Betrayal is nothing new. It's been on the scene from the beginning of time. And it has always been a crime committed from the inside. The Old Testament is full of prophecies and stories of betrayal.

- In the Garden of Eden, Eve betrayed Adam and both Adam and Eve betrayed God.

- Cain betrayed his brother, Abel, and committed the first murder recorded in the Bible.

- Jacob betrayed his brother, Esau, for his birthright.

- Joseph's ten brothers betrayed him, selling him into slavery.

- Absalom betrayed his father, David, to steal his kingdom.

- The Israelites betrayed God's love for them repeatedly, even going so far as to make idols and marry those God had forbidden them to marry.

- Delilah betrayed Samson to the Philistines.

The psalmist David wrote, "Even my close friend, someone I trusted, one who shared my bread, has turned against me"

(Ps. 41:9). Most likely, he wrote this around the time his own son Absalom and one of his counselors betrayed him. David was going through it himself:

> It is not an enemy who taunts me—I could bear that. It is not my foes who so arrogantly insult me—I could have hidden from them. Instead, it is you—my equal, my companion and close friend. What good fellowship we once enjoyed as we walked together to the house of God. Let death stalk my enemies; let the grave swallow them alive, for evil makes its home within them. (Ps. 55:12–15, NLT)

David's words were prophetic, foretelling what would happen to the Messiah, how He would be betrayed by one of His closest companions. Judas, the ultimate betrayer of Jesus, didn't just show up one day, as one of the hangers-on, and plant that kiss on the Lord. No, Judas was handpicked, chosen by Jesus to be one of His twelve disciples. He was one of the few, the intimate circle, privileged to travel with the Teacher and be part of His ministry. Jesus, knowing full well what Judas would do—the assignment Judas had been given in the gospel story—chose him to be part of His inner circle.

The Bible says that Jesus called Judas "the son of perdition" (John 17:12, KJV)—the only one of the twelve disciples who, from the beginning, was bent for destruction.

Betrayal will either kill you, slow you down, or force you to fix your eyes on what matters most.

If betrayal was part of Jesus' life experience, we are certainly not exempt.

There are people already in your life whose assignment, whose role it is to betray—to woo and win your friendship, your love and your trust and, when push comes to shove, turn on you as if you never meant anything to them. It is their assignment. They *will* fulfill it. And when they turn on you, their betrayal will hit you hard. There's no way around the devastating impact. Betrayal will either kill you, slow you down, or force you to fix your eyes on what matters most. It will force you to focus on whom or what you're really chasing after. Put another way, there will (eventually) be an up-side: Betrayal will grow you up!

The Real Judas

If you're like me, betrayal hits especially hard, because I'm a person who loves intensely. If you're in my circle, you're *in* my circle. And when you're in my circle that means I've got you. I've got your back. I've got your front. I've got you. I'm loyal to a fault . . . to the bitter end.

One of my friends told me I love so hard that God has to rip people out of my heart. Ouch! God has to rip them out because I'm all in, no matter what. Even when some people show me their true colors, I still want to believe in them. I'm the first person to say, "Nah, that's not really who they are. There must be some misunderstanding."

So staying in pursuit, how do you deal with betrayal?

In Ephesians 6:12, Paul makes it clear: "We are not fighting against flesh-and-blood enemies, but against evil rulers and authorities of the unseen world, against mighty powers in this dark world, and against evil spirits in the heavenly places" (NLT).

When it came time for Judas to betray Christ, the Bible says, "Satan entered Judas." Did you get that? Judas wasn't acting on his own. Satan was in the mix.

"Then Satan entered into Judas called Iscariot, who was of the number of the twelve. He went away and conferred with the chief priests and officers how he might betray him to them. And they were glad, and agreed to give him money. So he consented and sought an opportunity to betray him to them in the absence of a crowd" (Luke 22:3–6, ESV).

Commenting on this passage, eighteenth-century theologian Matthew Henry wrote:

> Christ knew all men, and had wise and holy ends in taking Judas to be a disciple. How he who knew Christ so well, came to betray him, we are here told; Satan entered into Judas. It is hard to say whether more mischief is done to Christ's kingdom, by the power of its open enemies, or by the treachery of its pretended friends; but without the latter, its enemies could not do so much evil as they do.[2]

Understand that this thing is spiritual. Betrayal isn't just a character flaw or a natural result of any number of very human actions. Betrayal is spiritual. It is a spiritual darkness. Betrayal is a devastating blow from within your inner circle planned by the Enemy to disrupt your desperation for God.

Paul wrote about this in his letter to the church of Galatia: "You were running a good race. Who cut in on you to keep you from obeying the truth?" (Gal. 5:7). When you're running after God, when you're seeking an intimate, ongoing relationship with Him, spiritual forces will come after you.

Joseph's brothers threw him down into a twelve-foot deep cistern and then *sold* him for twenty pieces of silver to slave traders. Joseph could've let his brothers' betrayal abort his dream, but he didn't. "You intended to harm me, but God intended it all for good," he told his brothers later in Egypt. "He brought me to this position so I could save the lives of many people" (Gen. 50:20, NLT).

> *When you're running after God, when you're seeking an intimate, ongoing relationship with Him, spiritual forces will come after you.*

Jesus could have detained Judas at that Last Supper, before Judas ever had a chance to run to those soldiers. In Matthew 26:23, Jesus identified Judas as His traitor: "The one who has dipped his hand into the bowl with me will betray me." *What?* That is so amazing. How do you stare into the eyes of the one you know is out to get you and not put your hands on them?

If ever a father loved his son, David loved Absalom. Yet, here's a boy who turned on his father so badly, so maliciously, it's heartbreaking to read. Granted, Absalom didn't have a perfect father. However, Absalom made his own choices. He chose to betray his father, scheming for years to win the favor of the people over his father. Not only did Absalom turn on David, but he led a conspiracy of others against David to steal his father's throne. It's the stuff movies are made of. Back in 2000, we all packed into movie theaters to see Russell Crowe in *Gladiator* and jeered at Commodus who murdered his father, Roman Emperor Marcus Aurelius, to gain the throne.

Even after everything Absalom did to his father, David told his soldiers, "If you see Absalom, don't kill him." When we love like that, we'll even try to save those who are out to destroy us, those who are set on destroying our spirits.

What Are You Looking At?

Once we understand that betrayal is a spiritual issue, directed by the Enemy and not necessarily by the person we know, we can better understand where our real focus should be.

We can weather betrayal when we have our eyes on Jesus. Yes, it's part of the chase, but it's also just another distraction keeping us from abundant life. Everyone who has ever had an encounter with God, everyone who is in pursuit of God, and everyone who is being used by God to accomplish anything will encounter betrayal. It's not a matter of *if* but rather *when*.

That's not to say it doesn't hurt. This kind of emotional pain cuts deep. I know. I've been there. But when we realize that the action is spiritual in nature, that the betrayer is fulfilling an assignment, we can begin to see the deeper meaning in it.

When Judas got up to leave, to go betray Christ, Jesus didn't run after Judas trying to stop him or convince him to stay. What did Jesus do instead? He continued to feast with the eleven brothers still seated around the table.

Unfortunately, most of us leave the table and run after the one who has betrayed us. Or, if we don't run after them, we focus so much on the one who hurt us, on the pain, rejection, and reality of the now empty seat around our table that we neglect to take stock of the loyal friends and family who are still "on our team."

I remember well when the Lord gave me that truth. I was reeling from the sting of betrayal. Someone I loved and trusted had left, and I was wallowing in the hurt. And the Lord clearly said to me, "Look around. Look who's still here. Look at the ones who are shielding and protecting you and who are praying for, covering, and loving you. Get your attention off the empty seat and celebrate the ones still sitting at the table."

Betrayers are on assignment. It's part and parcel of this journey we're on, to encounter obstacles—acts of spiritual darkness—that conspire to keep us from God. Just as betrayal was part of Jesus' journey to the cross, it's part of your journey, too. And until you can accept that, you'll keep on running after the Judas in your life. You'll stay focused on the hurt, pain, and broken promises they caused instead of focusing on the blessings right in front of you.

That's why Jesus' actions upon Judas' return are so important. Remember what Jesus did? When Judas came back with the guards, Jesus welcomed him, saying, "Do what you came for, friend." In other words, "Hurry up and do what you have to do so I can get to where I have to go—c'mon, kiss me. Come on, kiss me." When I finally "got" that, I stopped running after my betrayer and started celebrating who was around my table. I had more time to pour into the Peter's and the John's and the others sitting at the table. I had more time to be intentional and to love on the people still with me.

Remember this: When Judas left, John was lying on Jesus' chest. He was right there, faithful and constant and true. Sometimes we push away the faithful, devoted people in our lives to run after the Judas who has hurt us so badly. John, the disciple lying on Jesus' chest, was the one who would write Revelation. Judas wasn't going to write a thing. Like Jesus, you've got a Peter sitting at your table. You need to get him ready. You need to warn him that he's going to deny you in the moment and focus on his future redemption, rather than running after the one who's going to turn on you permanently.

Jesus knew what Judas would do. He knew the destiny of that man. And sometimes we don't want to admit it, but we know, too. Deep down, you know the traitor in your midst. You've seen the signs, and somewhere inside, you know. You know it can happen, and sometimes, you know when it's happening.

Some people are in your life for a reason, some are there for a season, and some people are in for a lifetime.

I always say that some people are in your life for a reason, some are there for a season, and some people are in for a lifetime. Some people are only going to be there for a while, and then they'll be gone. And then new people will be introduced. So your surroundings will change. Some of them will be there to take you further. Some of them will be brought in for you to bring them further. Always be clear on the assignment of the individuals who come into your life, into your circle. Some people will push you further; at times you'll need to be the one pushing someone else further. Keep that circle moving the way it needs to move.

So when it's time for someone to get off the train, slow your engines and let them off. Free the seat because someone else is expected to get on. That's the God-driven surrounding of people He has for you. We tend to struggle in that area because we don't like it when people exit our vision. But when their season is up, they need to exit.

Calling Your Judas

When you experience betrayal, tell your Judas to hurry up and do whatever they have to do, so you can get where you have to go. Just tell them to get on with it, so you can move on to the next thing God has for you.

I know firsthand that the prayer "God, give me the ability to call my Judas to kiss me" is a tough one. Our human nature wants to lash out at our Judas. Until you get that your Judas has been assigned to do something to you that will push you to another level, that prayer is almost impossible. We want to hit, to push away. The last thing we want to do is call over our Judas to "kiss" us.

Remember, Christ said that He was going somewhere, but He knew He couldn't get there without Judas. Someone had to do Him wrong. A lot of your wisdom, a lot of your life lessons, will come through pain. That's just the way it is. Wisdom and courage will come through people hurting you.

And yes, it's going to hurt badly, but keep that pain in perspective. It's not a nail; it's a splinter. That cross Jesus carried, it was full of splinters, but it would take more than splinters to kill Him . . . and a splinter won't kill you.

Even when we hurt, we can go to the Word. We must go to the source of our strength because this is a spiritual battle. The weapons of our warfare are not carnal, but of the Spirit, so we need to pray ourselves to that place where, like Jesus, we can say, "Father forgive them for they do not know what they are doing" (Luke 23:34). It isn't them. It's the battle for their spirit.

That's the hardest part, getting to the place of forgiveness. That's why Jesus says to forgive our neighbor not seven times but seventy-seven times (Matt 18:22). He knows that forgiveness, especially when we forgive someone who has betrayed our trust, is almost impossible. "Seventy-seven times" implies that forgiveness is an exercise to be practiced often, not for just select moments in our lives. That path to the place of "Father, forgive them" begins with the Spirit and brings us closer to the heart of God.

Few stories in our world today portray the power of forgiveness like those of the survivors of 1994's Rwandan genocide who have forgiven their Hutu neighbors who murdered and victimized them and their families. On April 7, 1994, a year after losing his mother to AIDS, Alex Nsengimana was five years old when Hutu militia came to his home, broke down the door, ordered him and his younger brother and older sister outside, and then killed his grandmother, the primary caretaker after his mother's death. Later, the soldiers returned and murdered the children's uncle right in front of them.

A year before the twentieth anniversary of the genocide, for the first time Alex met the Hutu man who killed his uncle. Over the years since his uncle's murder, Alex had struggled with learning to forgive these men who had killed his family.

"What I didn't want to accept is that [God] loved the guy who killed my uncle, and the guy who killed my grandmother," Alex told reporters. "And I lived in bondage for many years because of that."[3]

Contrast that with today. In his meeting with the man who killed his uncle, Alex shared a message of love and forgiveness, telling him that Christ came and died for him and that "[Jesus] loves him just as much as He loves me."[4]

In hindsight, Alex explained, "It was probably one of the toughest days of my life, but also one of my most freeing days because I was able to let go and was able to have the peace that only Jesus Christ can offer."[5]

Forgiveness is a powerful tool for overcoming betrayal because only through God's Spirit can we forgive like we're called to forgive.

Forgiveness is a powerful tool for overcoming betrayal because only through God's Spirit can we forgive like we're called to forgive. We can't do it in our human strength. In fact, it's impossible for the natural mind to understand the things of the Spirit. Our human spirit wants vengeance. We want justice for those who betray us. All of those human feelings are part of the process of becoming more like Jesus. Our desperate need for God's Spirit will keep us coming back in pursuit of an encounter with Him in prayer, in the Word, and in His presence.

We simply have to stay in the presence of God. We have no choice, because in His presence and in the refinement process, He purges us of us. He purges me of me. He purges you of you. In His presence is life. If we get tripped up by these spiritual potholes, we lose our desperation for Him. So understand that part of your journey, part of your pursuit, your desperation for God, is that bump in the road called betrayal. How then do you deal with it?

- Don't focus on the betrayal. Instead, accept it for what it is: an act of spiritual darkness. It happened. It is happening. And most likely, it will happen again.

- Don't run after your betrayer, chasing that person down, hoping to change or fix the situation, or keep it from happening.

- Identify and focus on those people who are still around the table. Celebrate the loving, devoted people who are still with you on the journey.

- Stay where you are. Stay in pursuit of God and keep moving forward.

- Pray yourself to the place of forgiveness and the freedom that letting go of anger and bitterness brings.

Jesus Christ had to make it to the cross. Joseph had to make it to Pharaoh's palace. And you have to keep your eyes on the prize.

A Desperate Prayer

Jesus, You know my heart is broken and my spirit wounded, but I pray that You will heal me. Help me to love and forgive those who have betrayed me just as You forgave the one who betrayed You. Please allow me to trust again and not hold this act against those who have done me wrong. Jesus, I pray as You prayed, "Father, forgive them for they know not what they do".

CHAPTER 6

THE POWERFUL PUNCH OF ANGER

W e all make mistakes. It's part of our DNA. And when we do, we get emotionally tangled up in the fall. It's hard to keep running after God, to continue pursuing Him with both your heart and mind, when you're tangled up, isn't it?

Anger is a tangled hot mess of emotion. It's natural, and it's going to happen. You're going to feel it, and sometimes with great cause. Here you are, running your own race, minding your own business, when someone cuts in on you. She spreads rumors about you. He takes credit for work you've accomplished. When you've been wronged in the chase, when someone cuts in on you, how is a true believer supposed to respond?

Scripture tells us there are two kinds of anger: righteous and unrighteous. How do you know the difference between each one? Author and theologian Warren Wiersbe identifies four criteria for righteous anger:

- Righteous anger is anger toward sin.

- Righteous anger is controlled by God, exemplifying strength and self-discipline.

- Righteous anger is concerned with defending and building up others rather than protecting our self-esteem.

- Righteous anger produces righteousness and not unrighteousness.[1]

Anger in itself is not evil or a sin. Anger can actually be a positive emotion. God created us with this emotion. But when left unchecked, fueled by pride, and not expressed in healthy and constructive ways, anger can destroy us. The Greek philosopher Aristotle once said, "Anybody can become angry—that is easy, but to be angry with the right person and to the right degree and at the right time and for the right purpose, and in the right way—that is not within everybody's power and is not easy."[2]

The Bible commands us to be angry but sin not: "'In your anger, do not sin': Do not let the sun go down while you're still angry" (Eph. 4:26). The New Living Translation interprets the same verse this way: "Don't sin by letting anger control you" (NLT).

Go ahead. Get angry. But don't sin.

One of the most significant examples in Scripture of getting angry but not sinning, or having righteous anger, is Jesus' response to the money changers in the temple. When Jesus entered the temple He found a market in what was supposed to be His Father's house of prayer (Matt. 21). He didn't just suggest they take their flea market elsewhere, He got angry. He flipped over their tables and forced out those money changers with a whip.

Now, understand why this was righteous anger. The temple leaders had allowed the holy place of God to become a hub of commercial activity. Because the temple dues were to be paid in Tyrian coins, and most people had only Jerusalem coins, most likely the temple-appointed money changers probably cheated or overcharged people who had traveled long ways to take part in the Passover celebration. So the atmosphere in the court of the Gentiles was like a flea market where merchants haggled with Jewish travelers and took advantage of them—keeping some who couldn't afford the high prices from taking part in the Passover, a significant celebration in the life of every Jewish person, and a celebration that should have been open to any Jewish person, not just the wealthy. Jesus' righteous anger was directed toward the sin of the temple establishment; His anger focused on defending others.[3]

Jesus was human, with emotions just like ours. But He didn't let His anger lead to out-of-character behavior. In other words, if anger isn't channeled correctly, it will act out. And if it acts out in negative ways, it can literally take you out. Check this out. Researchers have found that chronic anger is so damaging to the body that it ranks with, or even exceeds, cigarette smoking, obesity, and a high-fat diet as a powerful risk factor for early death. One study that analyzed the effects of chronic anger on women over a period of eighteen years found that those who had answered initial test questions with obvious signs of long-term, suppressed anger were three times more likely to have died than those who didn't harbor such hostile feelings.[4]

In the Old Testament, David provides an example of unrighteous anger in 2 Samuel—even though he mastered his anger and offered a model response to Michal's rebuke, as we saw earlier in this same story back in chapter 3. This is such a rich passage! When David set out to return the ark of the covenant to Jerusalem (2 Sam. 6), what happened? One of the oxen carrying the ark stumbled, and one of David's good, reliable men, Uzzah, reached up to keep the ark from falling to the ground. When he touched it, God struck him dead on the spot because he had defiled the ark. (God had given explicit commands to Moses and Aaron that *no one* was to touch the ark of the covenant and warned that doing so meant death. See Numbers 4:15.) At Uzzah's death, David boiled over with anger, and instead of moving on to Jerusalem, he stopped at someone else's house, stored the ark there, and waited. For three whole months, he was sidelined from bringing the ark of the covenant to his city. Anger, anger, anger!

Anger can stop us dead in our tracks. It can hold us back from accomplishing God's purpose. It can keep us from becoming desperate for Jesus. Once anger gets a small foothold, it wants to take over. Anger packs a powerful punch!

Moses had major anger issues. He let anger take over his actions and his words. When he saw the way the Egyptians were treating the Israelites (Ex. 2), he got so angry that he killed an Egyptian and hid his body in the desert. Fast-forward a few decades. Moses had freed the Israelites, and they were camped in the desert (Ex. 32). For forty days, Moses had been on the top of Mount Horeb, waiting for God to give him the commandment tablets. Finally, tablets in hand, he came down off the mountain, and what were his people doing? They were dancing and worshipping around a golden calf that Moses' own brother, Aaron, had helped them create. Moses got so angry he slammed the tablets to the ground—in his anger, he broke the handiwork of God.

Think about that! He intentionally destroyed the word of God. Moses' anger knew no boundaries.

He demanded the idol be destroyed and ground into powder. Then he forced the people to *drink* it. He was an angry man out of control! And then he told all of them, "Whoever is on the LORD's side, come over here with me. Get your swords and go back and forth through the camp and kill your brothers, friends, neighbors—basically anyone who is not on the LORD's/my side. I don't care if it's your mother or your little sister . . . kill them all" (see Ex. 32:26–28). *What?!* The Bible says that almost three thousand Israelites were killed that day.

There's not an anger management class in the world that could fix Moses' anger problem.

Later (Num. 20), even though God had been faithful to provide everything the Israelites needed to survive this long journey in the wilderness, an exasperated Moses lost his grip again. The land was dry. People were dying of thirst. The people were complaining (Num. 20:3–5, NLT):

> The people blamed Moses and said, "If only we had died in the LORD's presence with our brothers! Why have you brought the congregation of the LORD's people into this wilderness to die, along with all our livestock? Why did you make us leave Egypt and bring us here to this terrible place? This land has no grain, no figs, no grapes, no pomegranates, and no water to drink!"

The Lord's presence appeared to Moses and Aaron and told Moses, "Speak to that rock before their eyes, and it will pour out its water" (Num. 20:8). But an exasperated Moses didn't speak.

Instead, he took his staff, struck the rock, and yelled (v. 10), "Listen, you rebels, must we bring you water out of this rock?" I can just see Moses lifting that staff over his head and slamming it down on that rock: *Take that, you ungodly, ungrateful people! Ooh, that felt good. I think I'll do that again.* So he lifted that staff over his head again, crashing it down on the rock for a second time.

When we allow our anger to control us, consequences will follow. Moses' anger problem costs him dearly. The Lord told him, "Because you did not trust in me enough to honor me as holy in the sight of the Israelites, you will not bring this community into the land I give them" (v. 12). Seven chapters later, God said to Moses, "Go up on this mountain in the Abarim Range and see the land I have given the Israelites" (Num. 27:12). After all the years of wandering and struggle, God told Moses, "You can look at this place of promise, but you're not going to enter it." Moses was *this* close, and God said, "Go up on the mountain, look at the land that you're not going to set foot on."

When unrighteous anger consumes you to the point that it controls you, there will always be a high price to pay.

Kill the Anger Beast Before It Kills You

To be human is to feel anger. You're going to get angry . . . justifiably so. God created the emotion and feelings of anger. The question is, how do you process it constructively and eventually get rid of it?

To dispose of anger, we have to seize it. We have to grab hold of it, look it straight in the face for what it is, and find a way to shake it loose from us. If we have any hope of staying desperate in our pursuit of Jesus, we've got to put that anger beast down.

So how do we do that? As with so many of the obstacles we face in life—the experiences and emotions that interrupt our chasing after God—we need the right army, and we need the right weapon.

For the great evangelist and preacher Charles Finney, Daniel Nash was his army of one and his weapon was prayer. When God would direct Finney to the place for his next prayer meeting, Nash would slip quietly into that town to seek out two or three people to pray fervently with him for God to move in the community. Not only did Nash prepare the communities to hear Finney's preaching, he also continued in prayer during the meetings.

Often Nash would not attend meetings. While Finney was preaching, Nash was praying for the Spirit's outpouring upon him. Finney stated, "I did the preaching altogether, and brother Nash gave himself up almost continually to prayer."[5]

How many times have you walked through something only to find out later that several people in your life had been praying for you every day? That your name was being lifted up to the almighty God?

People and prayer. Everything comes down to surrounding yourself with the right people who will chase with you and immerse you in prayer—especially when you're dealing with something as lethal to your pursuit as anger.

For David, in 1 Samuel 25, Abigail was his army. David sent ten of his men to the house of a wealthy man, Nabal, to ask for food and drink. Now, David's men had protected Nabal's fields and shepherds for months, free of charge, but even so, Nabal refused to give them anything. When these ten men returned to David and told him that Nabal refused to offer them anything, David was livid. The Bible says he gathered up about four hundred men, *with swords strapped on,* to go kill Nabal and every man associated with him (v. 13, emphasis mine).

I completely understand why David was angry. Why wouldn't he be? David and his men had been more than kind to Nabal and his shepherds, even watching their stuff when they had to be away, and yet Nabal refused to give them food and drink after a long journey. And not only did he refuse these provisions, but he verbally insulted both them and David—humiliation on top of rejection!

> *We need people who can see the big picture and aren't afraid to get in our face and show it to us.*

To keep him from acting on his anger and killing Nabal and his men, David needed someone to step in and give him some perspective. Enter Nabal's wife, Abigail. Known throughout the land for her beauty and intelligence, Abigail acted quickly, packing a caravan of food, drink, and supplies for David and his men. When she got to David, she basically said to him, "Don't do what you're planning to do, David. You don't need to avenge the wrong that's been done to you. You don't need to answer wrong with more wrong. God will take care of it, and you will be blessed for letting it go."

A great tragedy was completely avoided because David had people around him who gave him a much-needed shift in perspective.

We all need a Daniel Nash or an Abigail in our lives. Someone who will pray for us, intervene for us, and talk us down off the ledge when anger—and other emotional obstacles—threaten to take our focus off the goal. When you get angry, you don't think rationally. When you're angry, everything else takes a back seat. The only thing in focus is what's in front of your face. You can't see the overall picture. You can't see the periphery, what's in front of you, or what's behind you. We need people who can see the big picture and aren't afraid to get in our face and show it to us.

One reason why the anger beast is so difficult to kill lies in that anger's heartbeat—the thing that births it and keeps it alive—is pride. Someone cuts you off, steals something, rejects or humiliates you, and it's a *right now* situation. Like David, you can't think about anything but what they've done to you and how fast and hard you can swing back. It's all about you and how you feel, and how you're going to deal with it. *Right now!*

With Moses, it was a *right now* situation. *These people are begging for water right now, and I'm going to get it out of this rock right now. Speaking to the rock is a waste of time; I'm taking this rock down in my own way.*

With David, we also see pride, front and center. *That surly Nabal refused and humiliated my men, so I'm taking 400 men back with me, and he's going to get what he deserves, right now!*

Each situation evokes an immediate response, a spark that in a matter of minutes—if not contained—becomes a raging fire. A blaze that must be put out before it burns everything up.

Be angry, but sin not.

Anger becomes a sin when it pushes you out of your pursuit, out of your desperation for God.

I can say this resolutely because I have been livid before. I have been angry. I have been mad. And I get so weary that I find myself having a little John Hannah conversation with myself in which I always win, they are always wrong, and I always have the last say. In your mind, you are always right.

It's a *right now* situation that wants you to react right now. But instead of reacting and giving in to the urgency, run to your secret place. Get alone with God so you can hear His Spirit.

Now contrast David's ire in the first two examples with how David dealt with anger in 1 Samuel 31. David and his men ravaged the Amalekites camp. Soon after, the Amalekites retaliated. David and his men returned to their camp in Ziklag and discovered the whole camp had been laid to waste and their wives and children taken into captivity. Devastated, David's people sat among the ruins, weeping for their missing loved ones. His men spoke of stoning David right there.

What did David do?

The Bible says he pulled back, separated himself from the people, and encouraged himself in the Lord. In other words, he got alone with God to pray and ask for guidance and wisdom. When he talked to God, he received instructions from Him.

Throughout Scripture, we see this pattern—prayer, the Word, and surroundings—repeated in the life of people in pursuit of God. Everything points back to these three.

God Has You Covered

If we learn to turn to God with our anger, before we react or act on it, He is faithful to save us from ourselves. Remember: His plan is to see us chasing after Him and finishing this race.

I often think about Peter and how angry he was when the guards came to arrest Jesus in the garden. He didn't think. Peter was angry, and he did what an angry man with a weapon does. He pulled out his sword.

Now keep in mind, Peter had been walking with Jesus for three and a half years. Why was he even carrying a sword? All this time with Jesus, in and out of crowds and boats and over rocks and hills, and Peter is walking around with a sword? So when he gets angry, you know what he's going to do. He did what you might do if you were in his shoes. He pulled out that sword and whacked off the ear of the high priest's servant Malchus. He commited a crime. Justifiable, maybe so, but still, a crime. In one angry instant, Peter became a criminal.

If we learn to turn to God with our anger, before we react or act on it, He is faithful to save us from ourselves.

Jesus couldn't allow that scenario to play out. Peter's anger was about to get him arrested, yet that couldn't happen. The book of Acts was waiting on Peter. Jesus had planned to pass the torch to Peter to carry it until Paul could be blinded on the road to Damascus and meet Jesus. Earlier, after Peter acknowledged Jesus as "the Christ, the Son of the living God," Jesus blessed him and said He would build His church on Peter: "Now I say to you that you are Peter (which means 'rock'), and upon this rock I will build my church, and all the powers of hell will not conquer it" (Matt. 16:18, NLT).

Jesus couldn't let Peter's anger get the best of him because Peter had to stay in the race and finish the course set before him.

So what did Jesus do? He reached up to Malchus' ear and healed it, as if nothing had happened. Jesus erased the criminal evidence so Peter avoided arrest. Yes, Jesus knew Peter's life would not be smooth sailing. Within hours, Peter would deny

Jesus repeatedly. Peter would soon have enough to deal with in forgiving himself for his denial. So Jesus had mercy on him, knowing that Peter had much to accomplish in His name.

And so it is with you and me. God has a plan for us, and anger that we allow to control us interrupts—and potentially destroys—His plan. But as He did in Peter's life, God covers us in our angry situations. Think about that. Think about a time when God covered you, despite the fact that you acted on your anger. He covered you, smoothing the aftermath of your anger so it didn't have long-term consequences, so it didn't completely knock you off the track in your pursuit of Him. He did that and continues to do that because He knows we're meant for bigger plans.

When You're Angry at God

As a pastor, I counsel with people in the most trying times of their lives. I've seen people experience things that would make anyone with a heart angry. Just this week, I sat with a mother whose son had a seizure on a bus, went into cardiac arrest and died. Out of the blue, dead at age thirty-one. I spoke with another couple struggling with infertility. They've had miscarriage after miscarriage, and they keep trying, while young unmarried women all around them seemingly get pregnant at the drop of a hat. They ask, "Why God? Why?"

Even in my own life, when my mom—the only real parent I had on this earth—was diagnosed with cancer and not even a year later died, I could've stayed angry and bitter at God for not healing her.

You will never be able to overcome your anger at God unless you understand that He is sovereign. Unless you understand how that word breaks down—that at the end of "sovereign" is the word "reign." Until you grasp that God reigns, that His ways are not our ways and that His thoughts are not our thoughts.

In 1956 while he, his wife, and their baby lay sleeping, white extremists bombed the Birmingham, Alabama, home of Dr. Martin Luther King, Jr. Only a man who believed and trusted in the sovereignty of his God could have responded to such violence in this way: "While I lay in that quiet front bedroom, I began to think of the viciousness of people who would bomb my home. I could feel the anger rising when I realized that my wife and baby could have been killed. I was once more on the verge of corroding hatred. And once more I caught myself and said: 'You must not allow yourself to become bitter.'"[6]

That night, King spoke and quieted the angered masses poised to retaliate for the bombing: "We are not advocating violence. We want to love our enemies. I want you to love our enemies. Be good to them. Love them and let them know that you love them."[7]

King's words hearken back two thousand years to Jesus' command to us all: "You have heard that it was said, 'You shall love your neighbor and hate your enemy.' But I say to you, love your enemies and pray for those who persecute you, so that you may be sons of your Father who is in heaven" (Matt. 5:43–45, ESV).

God's will, especially when it's completely beyond our human understanding, may leave us in emotionally vulnerable places—grief-stricken, confused, and angry. Still, we can accept and respond to our trials, knowing that He will never leave us alone. He will never leave us to drown in our grief. We don't have to let anger embitter us. He will always be there to help us work through every emotion, every obstacle in our way, in our desperate pursuit of true life in Jesus.

A Desperate Prayer

Father, Your word says, "Be angry but sin not." I ask that You help me to channel my anger in the right direction and not allow it to lead me into sin. Help me to remain in a peaceful place and not act out of character. Please give me the ability to rise above whatever has made me angry and speak to anger just as You spoke to the storm: "Peace, be still!"

CHAPTER 7

THE WEAKNESS OF SPIRITUAL IMMATURITY

One of the biggest obstacles to running desperately after God is simply the season of being a young lamb. Hopefully, it's a temporary season, but it's one we all go through.

Remember when you first got saved and started this new relationship with Jesus? You were on fire, especially if you were older and had already made major mistakes in life. The idea that your Creator could forgive you for the things you'd done and that you could start anew was just too much to take in. You were full of excitement and zeal about the new life you'd been introduced to.

But what happened a few weeks later when the real world hit? Some new Christians who try to do the Christian life on their own tend to do what sheep do when they're frightened or surprised. They wander off aimlessly. Without someone close by to help you walk the walk, to help show you the way and give you some accountability, at the very least your excitement will hit a brick wall of reality. Usually sooner than later, you realize that being a Christian doesn't exempt you from trials and obstacles.

Sometimes the church contributes to this misunderstanding, feeding new Christians a pipe dream that once they accept the Lord, everything will be perfect. Granted, when we're young in our faith, part of us needs to believe in that ideal. But in truth, life on this earth won't be a picnic for anyone. The Enemy has seen to that. Instead, like Ephesians 6:12 (*The Message*) says, this life is a fight to the finish:

> God is strong, and he wants you strong. So take everything the Master has set out for you, well-made weapons of the best materials. And put them to use so you will be able to stand up to everything the Devil throws your way. This is no afternoon athletic contest that we'll walk away from and forget about in a couple of hours. This is for keeps, a life-or-death fight to the finish against the Devil and all his angels.

I'll be the first to say that following Jesus in this world is a great challenge and even more difficult when you're young in the Lord. Even if you're fifty years old when you come to Christ, you're still just a child when it comes to knowing how to live in relationship with Him. Scripture tells us, "Do not think of yourself more highly than you ought" (Rom. 12:3). Sometimes, we think we're strong, especially when we're new in our salvation. We think we're more mature than we actually are. And then

Satan throws a curve ball, and we respond like toddlers, falling to the floor kicking, screaming, and pouting. Or we gather up our toys and run away from home. Because the real world has caved in on us and the Enemy has gotten in a good punch, we respond like children do when they don't get their way. We get mad and even run away. Immaturity wants what it wants right now. Immediately.

But we have to understand that not all the answers and solutions will be handed to us when we say "yes, Lord." In fact, Ecclesiastes 3:11 tells us we won't ever have all the answers regardless of our level of spiritual maturity: "He has made everything beautiful in its time. He has also set eternity in the human heart; yet no one can fathom what God has done from beginning to end."

That's why all of us have to be honest about what's happening in our lives—our struggles, failures, and faults. Wherever you're at in your relationship with Christ, you need to understand that following after Jesus is a process that will never be complete. We will always be chasing after Jesus. We will always be desperate to be closer to Him. Following Jesus is not a one-and-done proposition. Rather, it's a growing process of maturation that takes time.

Let me be clear, your salvation is final. That's finished. But as a disciple, you're part of an ongoing process. Think of how a person

> *Wherever you're at in your relationship with Christ, you need to understand that following after Jesus is a process that will never be complete.*

grows into an adult. When a baby is born, he is a living, breathing human being. That fact won't change. But this infant will grow into something more that we can't yet see. The body and mind he begins with will grow and mature. So will your faith.

In Luke 17, as Jesus was on His way to Jerusalem, ten lepers approached Him. They actually didn't come near Him. Instead, because they were "unclean" in the eyes of the law and forbidden to be near others, they all stood in the distance and shouted out to Him, "Jesus, Master, have pity on us!" But even when Jesus saw these men, they were not healed immediately. Instead, He told them, "Go, show yourselves to the priests." And the Bible says, "as they went, they were cleansed" (Luke 17:14). As they kept walking, they were healed. The spiritual life is a process we walk out.

Standing Tall on a Three-Legged Stool

To keep moving forward and growing in their faith, spiritually immature believers need the Word, prayer, and healthy surroundings. It's that three-legged stool—strong and balanced support for whatever life throws your way.

If you're a new believer, excited about growing in your chase, you should also be excited to spend time in God's Word, learning what it says about your pursuit of knowing Jesus. First Peter 2:2–3 says, "like newborn babies, long for the pure milk of the word, so that by it you may grow in respect to salvation, if you have tasted the kindness of the Lord" (NASB).

You crave the milk of God. And you should be getting plenty of it, jumping in with both feet and trying to absorb as much as possible. But just like a newborn baby (and sometimes a young toddler), you can't feed yourself. You must be fed.

I really believe that one of the perks of being new in the faith, of being spiritually immature, is realizing that you can't carry yourself. You must be carried. Until you can walk on your own, you need someone to help steady you and hold out arms of encouragement to keep walking. That's not a criticism or something to feel helpless or embarrassed about. All babies need their mamas, right?

When I first encountered God, He put people in my life like my grandmother and Edward Christian, who taught me His Word. He put people in my life like Elder Willie James Campell to show me, by example, how to live. People like the Mothers Board ladies prayer group who prayed over me and showed me how to pray. When you're young in the faith, you don't even understand prayer, so you must be prayed for. You have to learn what prayer is about and how to pray from other people more mature in the faith.

One thing's for sure, it takes that three-legged stool—the Word, prayer, and healthy surroundings—to grow you up as a believer. A two-legged stool is worthless. Maybe you're reading the Word and praying, but you haven't changed your surroundings. Or you're starting to change your surroundings but not spending time in the Word. Pull one leg out from underneath that stool, and it will all tumble down. When you're immature in your salvation and faith, you don't necessarily have these "legs" in place yet. That's why you need mature believers to steady you and hold you up as you grow in your faith.

It Is Written

I'm going to be upfront with you and just say it like it is: You won't find true, abundant life without God's Word. None of us will. You,

> *You won't find true, abundant life without God's Word. None of us will.*

me, your church-going, prayer-praying grandma . . . no one. Without His Word guiding our lives, we're living in our own strength.

Have you ever looked at Jesus' words in the gospels and realized how often He quoted Scripture? When Satan tested Jesus in the wilderness, Jesus continued to employ Scripture as His weapon against Satan's wiles. After Jesus was baptized and received the Holy Spirit (the dove came and rested on His shoulder), the Bible says He was "led by the Spirit into the wilderness to be tempted by the devil" (Matt. 4:1). After Jesus fasted forty days and forty nights, Satan came to test Him, and at each turn, what did Jesus say to Satan? Quoting Scripture from the Old Testament book of Deuteronomy, Jesus went back to Moses' encouragement and admonishments to the Israelites as they wandered in the desert:

- "If you are the Son of God, turn these stones into bread"/"It is written: 'Man shall not live by bread alone, but on every word that comes from the mouth of God.'" (Matt. 4:3–74; Deut. 8:3)

- "If you are the Son of God, throw yourself down"/"It is also written: 'Do not put the LORD your God to the test.'" (Matt. 4:6–7; Deut. 6:16)

- "All this I will give you if you will bow down and worship me"/"Away from me Satan! For it is written:

'Worship the LORD your God and serve him only.'"
(Matt. 4:9–10; Deut. 6:13)

Jesus resisted every temptation with specific Scripture. He knew the power of the Word, and even in His weakest moments He used that power to defeat the Enemy.

Spiritually immature people tend to fight Satan with their emotions, completely ignoring the powerful weapon ready for use. Remember Moses and what he did early in his walk with the Lord. Moses saw an Egyptian mistreating his people, and he committed murder. Moses acted in his emotions.

God's Word is powerful, sharper than any two-edged sword (Heb. 4:12). When you have the power of God's Word in your arsenal, hopeless situations are never hopeless. But you cannot use what you don't know.

When the Spirit placed the prophet Ezekiel in the valley of dry bones (Ezek. 37), the situation seemed hopeless. After all, how could Ezekiel bring those bones back to life? But God said to Ezekiel, "Prophesy. Speak to these dry bones." Immaturity tells us to get down in that valley and try to put those bones together ourselves. We act out of the limited understanding we have at the time. But Ezekiel, mature in the LORD, responded: "Dry bones"— *and here it is:* "Hear the word of the LORD" (v. 4).

When we begin to mature spiritually, we start to see how God's Word is integral to fighting the Enemy we'll inevitably face. We begin to seek out the Word before we act out of our emotions, and we start to see a God who through His Word brings dry bones to life.

On My Terms

When I first encountered God as an immature believer, I found out that someone had told a blatant lie against me. My pastor told me what had been said, but he cautioned me: "John, don't say anything. I just want you to know what you're dealing with."

What did I do? My immature self picked up the phone and called this guy: "I heard what you said about me." In that moment, I didn't care about the consequences. I was living in the *right now,* which is where we find ourselves when we're angry. I put my hands on it, and the situation went from bad to worse. When we take matters into our own hands, we can really make a mess.

Abraham and Sarah soon found themselves in a chaotic web of disobedience by taking control of a situation God had already handled. Talk about making a mess! In Genesis 16, after years of not being able to conceive a child with her husband Abraham, Sarah decided enough was enough. Even though God had promised that she and Abraham would have children—"offspring like the dust of the earth, so that if anyone could count the dust, then your offspring could be counted" (Gen. 13:16)—many years had passed since that promise, and Sarah was done waiting.

Taking matters into her own hands, she sent her Egyptian servant, Hagar, a pagan, to sleep with Abraham. She put her hands on something God already had control of. As a result, the rivalry between Sarah and Hagar and the sons they birthed, Isaac and Ishmael, respectively, created adversity and has fueled the Israeli-Arab conflict to this day. Galatians 4:23 says that Ishmael was born "according to the flesh" while Isaac was born "as the result of a divine promise."

That's what spiritual immaturity does. It makes you put your hands on things when you shouldn't, and you quit waiting on God. You try to make it happen your way, which is hardly ever a good idea.

One of the immaturities I see in new believers—especially among those who are young—is a rush to get married. They are in love and want to have sex, and they read in the Scriptures that it's better to marry than to burn with lust (1 Cor. 7:9). So they think, *I just need to go ahead and get married.* They take matters into their own hands and try to make it happen on their own terms.

Rushing into relationships, rushing into marriage, in order to deal with sexual desires, smacks of spiritual and emotional immaturity. You aren't thinking about the future, about the challenges of living in relationship with this person. Immaturity just says, *Why not get married?*

I've seen so many believers get knocked out of the race—out of this pursuit of God and the things of God—by marrying the wrong person because they were caught up in the idea of being in love and getting married.

If that's your situation—if you're months or years down the road in a marriage you prematurely jumped into—you need to hear this. *You can still choose to stay in the race.* In fact, if you married too quickly and didn't wait on God's promise, He can use that experience to intensify your pursuit of Him. Your situation may be difficult to deal with *without* becoming desperate for God. You'll need a continuous conversation with Him, His wisdom through the insight of His Word, and supportive surroundings in order to overcome the obstacles of your situation. If immaturity got you into marriage, then intensify your pursuit of Jesus to stay in it and in the chase.

The Now and the Not Yet

The Bible gives us so many examples and stories that speak to the importance of this maturation process, first and foremost the life of Jesus. It's amazing to think that Christ came to save the world, but God made Him wait until He was thirty to start His ministry. He probably felt ready at age nineteen or twenty, but it wasn't yet time. Even for Jesus.

Timothy was extremely young when Paul grabbed hold of him. Paul spoke to him as a father would speak to his son. He talked to him about being confident and being strong. With encouragement and a parental approach, Paul told him, "Timothy, you're going to do great things for God . . . in time."

Joseph was a young boy—the youngest of his brothers—when he first received the dream that he would rule, but he didn't sit in Pharaoh's court until he was thirty.

David was but a shepherd boy in his father's house—also the youngest of Jesse's sons—when he was called from the field into the house with Samuel. The Bible says that on that day, Samuel took the horn of oil and anointed him to one day be king of all of Israel in the presence of his brothers (1 Sam. 16:13).

After David received the anointing, he ended up playing the lyre to soothe King Saul's spirits (1 Sam. 16). After David slayed Goliath (1 Sam. 17), great things happened to him and terrible things happened to him. He won big, and then Saul chased him out of the palace. David made good decisions, and he made bad ones. But through it all, he kept running . . . he kept moving . . . he kept his pursuit. He ran through his season of immaturity until he finally sat on the throne.

During all the ups and downs, God put people in David's path who were there to help him keep moving forward. The Bible says Jonathan loved David "as his own soul" (1 Sam. 18:3, ESV) and was his covenant friend in Saul's palace. But later, when David escaped to the Cave of Adullam (1 Sam. 22), God gathered others around David to aid him on his journey. David's brothers and others from his father's house came to join him, and the Bible says, "All those who were in distress or in debt or discontented gathered around him, and he became their commander. About four hundred men were with him" (1 Sam. 22:2). So while living in that dark, damp cave, David's brothers came to him, and then four hundred men came and joined him, and he became their commander.

Interesting, isn't it? Jesus was born to bear the cross for our sins and show us how to live, but He would not start his ministry until age thirty. Both Joseph and David were appointed to rule, but it would be years before they assumed their ultimate leadership positions. They weren't ready for it. They were too immature. They had to live through a lot of life lessons before they would be ready. There was a process to go through, paces to walk. Immaturity is thinking that just because you've been appointed or called to something, you get it now.

I know what that feels like. I was in my early thirties, and I wasn't a senior pastor yet, though I had apprenticed with several. I knew I had been called to pastor a church, and in my immaturity, I remember crying out and telling God, *You've forgotten about me.* Not wanting to wait on God and determined to get my way, I applied for a ministry position and was called to interview at a church. When I pulled up into the parking lot, the Holy Spirit spoke to me and said, *This is not for you.* He warned me, *You are about to give this board permission to make a decision over your destiny and your assignment. Don't go in there, John.* It was clear as day.

But being immature, I can say in retrospect, I overrode the Spirit's leading and went right in. And that board spoke down to me. They degraded me. When I came out, I heard the Spirit say, *What did you expect? You went into the Enemy's camp. I didn't send you in there.*

Immaturity can cause us to get off-focus, to veer all over the place, willy-nilly, like we don't have any real grounding. It takes life experience, the maturing process, to get our real footing.

In track and field events, a false start—coming out of the running blocks before the sound of the gun—forces a yardage penalty. The big leagues, however, have a zero-tolerance policy. If a runner starts too soon, he or she is automatically disqualified from the race. Everything they've worked for is gone in a split second.

In August 2011, Olympic champion Usain Bolt came to the World Athletics Championships in Daegu, Korea, prepared to defend his 100-meter world record, establishing his "world's fastest man" status even further. The short stretch of 100 meters was Bolt's signature race. A year earlier in Berlin, Germany, the Jamaican-born athlete quickly came out of the starting blocks and almost effortlessly crossed the 100-meter finish line in 9.58 seconds, breaking his own time of 9.69 seconds in the 2008 Olympics by eleven hundredths of a second. No doubt, the 100-meter event had become Bolt's event.

So when he arrived in Korea after his stunning performance in Berlin, Bolt was a shoe-in for the champion's podium and possibly another 100-meter world record. On Sunday, August 28, 2011, before the anxious crowd of thousands who had gathered for the finals of the 100-meter race, Bolt entered the starting blocks poised for greatness. A few seconds later, instead of floating across the finish line as expected, a devastated Bolt slapped a wall in anguish, his gold and green running vest pulled up over his face. Bolt had committed the cardinal sin in track. He had left the blocks early. He was quickly disqualified and left the stage he had dominated since the 2008 Beijing Olympics empty-handed.

Bolt wasn't the only casualty of the unforgiving zero-tolerance policy. The day before his 100-meter event, meet officials had to escort 2008 Olympic champion Christine Ohuruogu off the track after false starting in a preliminary round.[1]

Just like Bolt and Ohuruogu felt the fatal sting of what happens when a runner literally jumps the gun, getting ahead of God—not waiting on Him and running ahead of His plans and promise—has consequences. Thankfully, our God doesn't have a zero-tolerance

When our spiritual immaturity keeps us from trusting God and His Word, and when we act on that impatience, life can get messy and just plain sad.

policy. We can come to Him for forgiveness and a new start. But no doubt about it, when our spiritual immaturity keeps us from trusting God and His Word, and when we act on that impatience, life can get messy and just plain sad.

Spiritual immaturity can make us run ahead of God, not allowing us to truly seek Him. In fact, immaturity often doesn't take into consideration that we're in a chase, and that the chase is not a sprint. Immaturity makes you run faster and faster, when maturity says *pace yourself.*

But how do you avoid this very thing that comes so naturally to young believers? Scripture says we are to build up our faith, praying in the Holy Spirit. You stay in the Word. You learn to pray. You surround yourself with mature Christians who can speak truth into your life. And in all of these pursuits, you listen for the Holy Spirit. Jesus said, "When he, the Spirit of truth, comes, he will guide you into all the truth" (John 16:13). Learning to wait on God requires us to be totally dependent upon His Holy Spirit.

There is a level, a place in your life and ministry where people are only going to use you for your fishes and loaves— what they can get from you. Then there's another place, another level, where you'll be equipped to deal with the Pharisees and the Sadducees, the naysayers. You'll have to attain a certain level of maturity to understand and overcome the fact that your family doesn't understand you and your beliefs. You'll need some perspective and maturity to sit with your Judas, knowing that he's going to walk out and turn you over. There's a place in your spiritual maturity you'll need to be at to wash the feet of Peter, who's going to deny you later. A spiritually immature person could never wash his betrayer's feet. He'd twist their ankle.

You know what I did after that discouraging interview? I settled into New Life Covenant on the north side of Chicago, and I didn't take another interview. I waited on God. I didn't plant my church until I was forty years old. And when I did, I planted New Life Covenant Southeast out of Pastor Choco's church. I'm so grateful that God didn't give me this church in my twenties or my thirties. I couldn't have handled it. I wasn't ready. My heart and head needed time to go through a process to become the leader God had in mind.

Growing in faith, in relationship with God, is a process. It takes time. You can't do and be all you think you should do and be when you're an immature believer. You can't handle everything you think you can handle.

The Voice of the Spirit

Immaturity means that you will make some mistakes, but when you do, expect to be disciplined. The Bible says the Lord chastises those whom He loves (Heb. 12:6). Maturity allows you to take your chastisement and stay in the chase. Maturity allows you to stay because you can see that God's correction is all for your good.

Immaturity should keep you in pursuit of God. Joshua would be the one to actually lead the children of Israel into the Promised Land. He had to stay close to Moses. He remains a minor character in Moses' story until we get to Joshua 1, where three or four times God said to Joshua, "Okay, son, so Moses is now dead." He said to him several times—and you can only speak this to a mature person—"Be strong and courageous. You're not a kid anymore." God was talking to a spiritually mature man now, not a boy.

Think about this: When David was called out of the field and anointed as the next king of Israel, the Bible says Samuel "anointed him in the presence of his brothers, and from that day on the Spirit of the LORD came powerfully upon David" (1 Sam. 16:13). God's Spirit was with David in this immature state from that day forward, because David was going to need the Spirit to go up against Goliath. He would need the Spirit to deal with Saul. Dependence on the Holy Spirit would be essential when he had to run from Saul. David needed the Spirit because in the natural, none of those obstacles would be possible to overcome—only in and through the Spirit.

Thank God, our immaturity doesn't keep the Holy Spirit at arm's length. Thank God we aren't under a zero-tolerance policy. He is loving, kind, and faithful, full of mercy and grace for us, especially when we're young and immature. His ways are not our ways, and His thoughts are not our thoughts. Thank you, Jesus.

A Desperate Prayer

Father, I thank You that You are forever patient with me as I grow into the person You have called me to be. Please teach me not to me anxious for anything and to know that I am growing at Your pace. I thank You that seasons change and that every season of immaturity has been a learning experience. I'm grateful for the testimony that I will have when I graduate out of the season of spiritual immaturity. Glory to God!

CHAPTER 8

THE PURSUIT
OF THE FLESH

A s if all these obstacles weren't enough—hard times, relationships, anger, betrayal, and spiritual immaturity— there's one hindrance that's always with us. We are all bound in this flesh—our human nature.

The sheer picture of being bound up tells us we can't fight. Until you realize that you're wrapped up in the enemy of the flesh, you're fighting a losing battle. Your human nature will *never* drive you toward God or encourage you to immerse yourself in His Word. Your flesh craves what it's made of, this earth. Our flesh is in search of earthly pleasures and pursuits, not spiritual things.

In Romans, Paul reminds us that "no good thing" dwells within our flesh: "For I know that nothing good dwells in me, that is, in my flesh. For I have the desire to do what is right, but not the ability to carry it out" (Rom. 7:18, ESV). In the New Testament, we see the word *flesh* used in multiple ways. Often, Scripture uses the word to refer to the mind, emotions, temperament, and physical body—the elements of our makeup. Never does the flesh refer to something spiritual.[1] Jesus separates the two in John 3:6 (ESV): "That which is born of the flesh is flesh, and that which is born of the Spirit is spirit."

The apostle Paul makes it clear that the flesh and the spirit are at constant war with each other: "For the desires of the flesh are against the Spirit, and the desires of the Spirit are against the flesh, for these are opposed to each other, to keep you from doing the things you want to do" (Gal. 5:17, ESV).

Our flesh wants absolutely no contact with God. The flesh can't stand in God's presence. It fights against what the Spirit wants. In fact, the moment that our flesh gets in the presence of Jesus, it buckles and submits.

But we humans, we're messed up, so we lean on our own human understanding and trust our flesh. We actually *trust* the enemy. And when we trust our flesh, we end up giving it what it wants. Our flesh demands so many things. When we feed our flesh what it demands, the enemy within succeeds in pulling us away from God.

Why would you trust your flesh? Think about this: When you die, your flesh will go back to the dust from whence it came. But it will drop your soul off in hell. Your flesh will carry your soul straight to hell and say, "Well, I'm not going."

I've seen so many people feed their flesh and kill their future.

I knew a young man in college who was a virgin when he got to campus. He was one of the most amazing young men. Totally anointed. He could pray. He could sing. He had so much potential for ministry. But at college, if you don't keep your focus, you'll be swept away by the culture, by the flesh, and by the flesh's demands. He decided he needed to get rid of his virginity. And when he opened that can, his flesh took over. He's dead now. He died of AIDS. The enemy within took everything.

Yet sometimes when we give in to the flesh, it doesn't take everything. Instead, it leaves us with a load of guilt, shame, and condemnation that hinders our pursuit of God. Satan uses the flesh to lie to us and convince us that God doesn't want us or can't forgive us now that we've messed up. Sometimes, he uses the flesh to convince us we can be like God.

Make no mistake, the flesh is a boldface liar that's hunting for our very lives and souls. The Bible says, "Be alert and of sober mind. Your enemy the devil prowls around like a roaring lion looking for someone to devour" (1 Peter 5:8).

So How Do We Slay the Enemy?

If we have any hope of controlling the enemy within—our flesh and what it wants—we have to be intentional and disciplined. Saying no and committing ourselves to live disciplined lives should be part of our daily routine.

Believe me. I know. At college, I had only been saved for a few months when I arrived on campus. So you can probably imagine how it was, being a young man, living on my own for the first time in my life amidst all that peer pressure. I didn't get married until I was twenty-nine. You think I had to learn the hard way to say and practice "no"? I certainly did. Nothing about it was easy.

Denying my flesh had to become my way of life. In that environment, there was no other way to stay the course God had called me to. And in that day and time, as it is today, no one wanted to deny himself anything. Our human nature doesn't even know *how* to deny itself.

But Jesus says, "If any of you wants to be my follower, you must turn from your selfish ways, take up your cross, and follow me" (Matt. 16:24, NLT). Notice what happens first? Denial of self. Following Christ, pursuing a relationship with Him, means you live a self-denial kind of life—a lifestyle of dying to self.

Make no mistake. A life of self-denial is just plain hard.

People look at me now and they say, "Oh, you're so blessed," but they don't know the long trail of denying my flesh. I dated a young lady one time. I really liked her. And she wanted to cross that line. She was ready, willing, and able, and there I was, a healthy young man, saying, "I can't. I can't." I wasn't willing to give up everything that God had for me. I just couldn't. And it's not just sex. So many other temptations came along, temptations that looked like opportunities—opportunities that looked good and would have felt good to the flesh.

I had a job opportunity one time, a position that anyone would've jumped at. It had all the bells and whistles, and it would have made me look accomplished and important. The job came with a high-rise office in downtown Chicago, complete with a spectacular view of the skyline and Lake Michigan. It was everything a young man could want.

But the Spirit told me, "No, that's not your job." Many times what looks great to everyone else isn't right for you according to the Spirit. That's how Satan got Eve in the beginning: one shiny piece of fruit. The Bible says when she looked at the fruit, it was pleasing to her eye (Gen. 3:6). And that's the way it is: So many things look good to the eye, to the flesh, but they're not good for our souls.

If our deepest desire is to pursue God and His purposes in our lives, we must surrender our flesh and do it daily. Because there is enmity between it and God, our flesh must die daily to the Spirit.

The apostle Paul continually spoke and wrote about dying and being raised in Christ, always in the sense that though we are a new creation in Christ—and that's final—dying to our flesh is a continuing process. In his first letter to the church of Corinth, Paul wrote, "I face death every day" (1 Cor. 15:31). As followers of Jesus, we have to learn to surrender our flesh, not to trust it, but to control it—before it destroys us. Like Paul says, we've got to die—*every day* that we get up. Every day, we have to fight to not give our flesh what it wants.

If our deepest desire is to pursue God and His purposes in our lives, we must surrender our flesh and do it daily.

What does it really mean to die to our flesh? When we think about physical death, the body dies and ceases to live. A person is said to no longer exist. In the same way, when we die to self spiritually, self ceases to exist. In Galatians, Paul paints a vivid picture: "I have been crucified with Christ and I no longer live, but Christ lives in me" (Gal. 2:20). When Christ lives in us, our wants and desires progressively shift from being self-centered to God-centered and others-centered. We increasingly understand and grasp that

God has created us for something more than earthly pursuits, to glorify Him as He uses us for His purposes. Paul says we are "God's handiwork, created in Christ Jesus to do good works, which God prepared in advance for us to do" (Eph. 2:10).

Chasing after Jesus is an ongoing process of dying to self and living for Christ, seeking His will rather than our own. And in that process, we discover the end goal—true life with Jesus— knowing, trusting and believing that He has created us for far more than we can imagine or fathom, namely a relationship with Him here in this life and when we meet Him face to face.

Known for his great faith and ministry to more than 10,000 orphans, nineteenth-century English evangelist George Müller was once asked the secret of his devoted service to the Lord. Müller answered, "There was a day when I died, utterly died." As he spoke, Müller bowed down, nearly touching the floor. "[I] died to George Müller—his opinions, preferences, tastes and will—died to the world . . . died to the approval or blame even of my brethren and friends—and since then I have studied only to show myself approved unto God."[2]

The most difficult prayer to pray is, "Not my will, but Thine be done." We didn't come into this world seeking God and desiring to be others-centered. But as followers of Christ, dying to self and killing the flesh are not options.

> *The most difficult prayer to pray is, "Not my will, but Thine be done."*

When I was a teenager, I started smoking cigarettes. I loved everything about it. Smoking was the coolest thing—to just sit there all laidback, light up, and smoke that cigarette. It made me feel large and in charge. But when I accepted Christ, the Spirit said, *Okay, let's get rid of the cigarettes.* I loved cigarettes so that was hard to swallow. But the Spirit said, *No. It doesn't go with your destiny. It doesn't go with what I have planned for your life.*

That's what denying your flesh is about. It's about listening for the Spirit and surrendering the things your flesh wants and craves for something better. I love what the German evangelist Dietrich Bonhoeffer said in his great work, *The Cost of Discipleship:* "We have to practice strictest daily discipline; only so can the flesh learn the painful lesson that it has no rights of its own."[3]

Knowing the Voice

Killing the flesh is simply not possible without knowing the voice of the Spirit. You can't live this life without it. We are led of God's Spirit. In the gospel of John, Jesus called Himself the Good Shepherd, saying, "I know my sheep and my sheep know me" (John 10:14). Moreover, the sheep follow the Good Shepherd "because they know his voice" (John 10:4).

We have to learn—in the heat of the chase—to listen and recognize the voice of the Spirit. Along the way, you'll have questions, but you learn and stay the course to know Him more . . . to know His voice.

When New Life Covenant Southeast was young and growing, I needed someone to talk to. So I prayed for a confidant, someone to mentor me, someone I could talk to about the ministry and about where I was, spiritually speaking. Bishop Arthur Brazier was an older gentleman here in Chicago who was a major pillar in the African-American community, and he had one of the largest churches in the city, from which he had retired. I prayed for someone to talk to, and God made a way for me to be in the same room with Bishop Brazier.

So we get in a room, and he says, "I know who you are, and I've been waiting on you." We ended up talking for almost two hours, and I remember to this day what he told me. He said, "There are three vices I want you to look out for, three vices that will destroy your ministry if you're not careful: pride, money, and women. These tantalizing vices will come in and take you out."

"Women will come on to you," he told me. "They don't want you. They only come to destroy your ministry. Money can destroy you. Don't live a lifestyle above your means. Remember you are a servant. And pride: never believe the hype. Never."

I remember his words like he spoke them yesterday. It was like the Lord said, *I want you to really get this, so listen carefully to this man.* About eighteen months after Bishop Brazier spoke to me, he died. But I'm so grateful that God put that man in my life to just pour into me and speak God's wisdom to me.

When you begin to see the signs or the validation of your obedience in surrendering what your flesh wants to what the Spirit says, your heart becomes even more attuned to the Spirit's voice. Daily dying to self and listening for the Spirit's direction, we give up everything of the flesh to know Him more.

It has always been this way for those who would follow God.

Shadrach, Meshach, Abednego, and Daniel refused to eat the king's meat or drink his wine. They surrendered everything, and God delivered them.

Once a persecutor of Christians, Saul (later Paul), who met Jesus on the road to Damascus, had to deny everything he had learned, everything he was: a commander, a ruler. He had to walk away from all of that.

When David ran from King Saul, he took nothing. He left everything behind.

Then there's the original disciples of Jesus who left their families and gave up everything to follow Him. Historians believe that all of the disciples except John and Judas died martyrs' deaths to follow Jesus. Peter was crucified head down at his own request (he felt unworthy to die in the same way as his Master). James was put to death by Herod Agrippa. Andrew is reported to have been crucified on an x-shaped cross. Thomas died by lance. Matthew, Jude, and Simon the Zealot are said to have died martyrs. Philip was crucified, Bartholomew was skinned alive and beheaded. James the Lesser was stoned and clubbed to death while James the Greater was beheaded.[4]

And yet we live in a world where no one wants to deny themselves anything.

Still, to live desperate for Jesus is to deny ourselves. There's just no way around it. The more you chase after Him, the more you lose interest in what this world has to offer, and the less you want to be yourself. You seek Him instead. The more you seek Jesus, the more like John the Baptist you will become: "He must become greater; I must become less" (John 3:30). When you become desperate for Him, for His will, and for His Word, you will begin to see His hand in your life in ways you never envisioned. When you look in

The more we focus on Him, the more our hearts will want to be like His and the more natural self-denial will become.

the mirror, you see not who you were in the flesh, but rather the person He's recreating in you. A new creation.

The more we focus on Him, the more our hearts will want to be like His and the more natural self-denial will become. We willingly deny ourselves, knowing that what God has for us is beyond anything we could get in the flesh.

The Ugh of You

Before we can get to that state of living in surrender, though, we have to exit the immaturity state. Immaturity makes denying self seriously difficult. Until we understand the ugliness of our humanity, we walk around on autopilot, doing what comes naturally. Until you get that *ugh* about yourself, you're going to fulfill you. You're going to live in the flesh. You'll never be able to die to yourself unless you're convinced that serving the flesh is of absolutely no worth.

It's not a self-loathing issue. I'm not saying hate yourself. I'm saying I can't imagine living as John Hannah based on John Hannah's ideas and desires. I want to be who God wants me to be, not who John Hannah can be on his own. I want to be more like Jesus. That's what I'm running after. I'm desperate for Him. He tells us in the gospel of Matthew, "Seek first his kingdom and his righteousness, and all these things will be given to you as well" (Matt. 6:33). If I get fame or fortune as I'm chasing more of God, that's only a benefit—it's not an identity. And it's certainly not my focus. Without Him, fame and fortune are miserable.

When people chase fame and fortune, believe me, that's a road to destruction. We've all seen where that leads. I've seen people in ministry who became famous and then went after the fortune. And I've seen them crash and burn because they're like King Nebuchadnezzar—who became proud and puffed up, taking credit for the kingdom that in reality God had given him: "Is not this the great Babylon I have built as the royal residence, by my mighty power and for the glory of my majesty" (Dan. 4:30)? The Bible says from that day, Nebuchadnezzar's nails became like claws, his hair grew like feathers, and he ran through the wilderness like a wild man.

That's what happens when our flesh seeks its own reward, seeks to glorify itself. We lose what we're running after. When we kill the flesh, we gain perspective, purpose and the power of the Spirit—to help us die to self. God gives sufficient grace to those who fight the good fight: "If you remain in me and my words remain in you, ask whatever you wish, and it will be done for you" (John 15:7). Yet another reason to continue in our chase for God and His glory.

Our focus must be on prayer, the Word, and our surroundings. I've seen it over and over again in my ministry: you can't do this on your own. You can't surrender your flesh and die to yourself every day without these three essentials keeping you on the path. Prayer must be paramount, followed by God's Word, and the people He places in your life. Jesus never sent the disciples out alone. When He released them, He sent them out in teams and said, "Gird yourselves up with the sword of My Word." Everybody needs others to keep them on the path. Pray for it. God will send you the person you need.

If we're pursuing God—surrendering our flesh and its need for power and success to the One who makes all things new and perfect—He gets all the glory. We don't want or need the credit for anything we accomplish by His Spirit. We're constantly pointing to Him. If we're desperate to be more like Him, if we're living lives of self-denial, we're constantly pointing to the One we're running toward.

The Flesh Won't Forgive, but God Does

What I love about God is that even when we mess up, He's there to clean up our mess and to get us back into the chase.

- Abraham doubted God and took matters into his own hands (flesh), and God was silent for thirteen years. But when at last God spoke to Abraham, God gave him a new name, a clean slate, and confirmed His covenant with him (Gen. 17).

- Moses responded out of anger and killed the Egyptian soldier (flesh) before God called him back by the burning bush (Ex. 3).

- David messed up with Bathsheba (flesh), even making sure her soldier husband died in battle, and thought he had gotten away with it. But the prophet, Nathan, called him out and got him back in pursuit of God (2 Sam. 12).

- Elijah wound up depressed in a cave, and God called him out to see His presence (1 Kings 19).

How do you think Peter felt? Three times, he denied that he knew Jesus the night of Jesus' arrest—just like Jesus said he would. The rooster crowed, and Scripture tells us that Jesus looked Peter straight in the face after the third time. Peter went into major depression.

What happened then? Jesus had been crucified, and the disciples were gathered in the upper room when the resurrected Jesus appeared to them. Peter stood in the corner, full of guilt, shame, and self-condemnation. Jesus walked through the doors, spoke to the disciples, and said nothing about Peter's denial. It was over and done.

But then Peter—*here it is:* went back to fishing. Did Jesus not say to him the first time they met, "Drop your nets and follow me"?

Peter was back on a boat, fishing—the very thing Christ had called him out of. He wasn't just back on the boat; he was there without his tunic. He was naked. Still, Jesus shouted to Peter from the shore. *Giving into the flesh will drive you back to an old lifestyle.*

Even when we've messed up royally, Jesus still comes to get us. We just have to make it through that season of guilt, shame, and condemnation. Responding to Jesus' call, Peter immediately jumped up, put on his clothes, threw himself into the sea, and swam to Jesus. The Savior of the world invited the disciples, "Come and have breakfast with Me." He had a fire going with fish already on it. Jesus had a breakfast date with the disciples, and He spoke into Peter's life to get him back on course. Remember, Peter had to get back on track, back in the chase, because the book of Acts was coming up, and Jesus had already said Peter would lead His church. Again, at the breakfast, Jesus made no reference to Peter's denial. Keep in mind that these are the first words Jesus has said to Peter since before His trial and crucifixion. I love this. Jesus said to Peter:

"Do you love me more than these?"

"Lord, you know I love you," Peter answered.

Don't miss this: Peter's love for God was deeper than his mistake. We may not realize it, but our love and desire for God are so much deeper than the mistakes we make, or the fleshly demands we give in to. Jesus knew Peter loved Him, but He asked anyway. And when Peter answered as Jesus knew he would, Jesus replied:

"Then get up—get up and tend my sheep." In other words, *get up and get back in this chase. Get back in pursuit.*

Jesus asked him again, "Peter do you love me?"

"Lord, you know I love you," Peter replied.

"Then get up."

Now Peter knew why Jesus had told him, before his arrest and the denial, "Simon, Simon, Satan has asked to sift all of you as wheat. But I have prayed for you, Simon, that your faith may not fail. And when you have turned back, strengthen your brothers" (Luke 22:31–32). In hindsight, Peter realized how easily he fell— and how deep was the forgiveness of his Savior. He also realized he had a new assignment in light of his failure.

We're going to fail, but when we confess our sin and ask forgiveness, we'll come back stronger—and when we do, Jesus says we have a responsibility to come alongside others in their chase.

There's no need to address it anymore, Jesus says to us. Whatever you've done in your flesh is done. I've moved on. Why keep rehashing and reliving and beating yourself up over what's done? Let go. Let's get back on the path of pursuit.

Pastor and author Bill Kynes compares our reluctance to move on from our sins to the American slaves after the Civil War. These slaves had received their emancipation, but some had lived their whole lives as slaves and didn't know what it meant to live as free people. They still thought they could be bought and sold as property. "So many times, we act like freed slaves, under the reign of sin," Kynes writes, "when in fact we died to sin, and we are now under God's grace.[5]

Colossians 1:13 tells us that the Father "has rescued us from the dominion of darkness and brought us into the kingdom of the Son he loves." We are forgiven and have new life in Him. Paul tells us, "Sin will have no dominion over you" (Rom. 6:14, ESV).

In *Mere Christianity,* what some theologians consider to be C. S. Lewis' finest work, Lewis writes: "A Christian is not a man who never goes wrong, but a man who is enabled to repent and pick himself up and begin over again after each stumble—because the Christ-life is inside him, repairing him all the time, enabling him to repeat (in some degree) the kind of voluntary death which Christ Himself carried out."[6]

By recognizing the flesh as the enemy, voluntarily dying to self as Christ did for us, embracing the Spirit's guidance, and living in the freedom and power His forgiveness offers, we come out of darkness and into light. And in the light, in His glorious presence, my friend, is where you will find true life.

A Desperate Prayer

Lord, I pray that I might decrease as You increase in my life. Please help me to crucify my flesh every day and not feed it what it craves. Teach me to live a life of sacrifice and denial of my flesh. Your strength is made perfect in my weakness, so please be strong in my weakest moments. Never let me feed the flesh to the point that it destroys Your will for my life. Help me Lord!

PART 3

A LIFE OF DESPERATION

CHAPTER 9 | **THE FRUIT OF DESPERATION**

ave you ever thought that a life of desperation to know Jesus brings fruit? Jesus said that when we abide in Him, we will bear much fruit.

> If you abide in me, and my words abide in you, ask whatever you wish, and it will be done for you. By this my Father is glorified, that you bear much fruit and so prove to be my disciples. (John 15:7–8, ESV)

The fruit of desperation identifies us as His disciples or "learners." The word *disciples* was originally a Greek word (μαθητὴς) meaning "learners." When we desire to abide in Jesus, to be like Him, we are filled during that process, and He changes everything. He changes the way we think, the way we see things, the way we respond to hard times. He changes the way we live. As John the Baptist said, as He increases, we must decrease. We are now the light—a city on a hill that cannot be hid (Matt. 5:14)—in the midst of darkness.

We're born into sin and shaped in iniquity, but when we have an encounter with Jesus—and begin our chase—we are transformed and begin to walk in the newness of life that Jesus promises. The fourth of the Beatitudes—a collection of Scriptures citing eight characteristics of what it means to be blessed—tells us, "Blessed are those who hunger and thirst for righteousness, for they will be filled" (Matt. 5:6). Did you catch that? As Jesus spoke to His disciples, He compared our longing for righteousness to a starving man desperate for food and water, desperate to live. When our longing is as intense as that, we will be "filled" or "satisfied" (ESV).

When we're truly chasing after Him, we begin to see people as God sees them. We start to see His power and Word unleashed in our lives and in the lives of others, and we see Him graciously fulfill our vision. God is so gracious as to write us into the redemptive story He's telling.

As He Sees Them

Earlier, I told you about Mother Davis, the woman my friends met in the grocery store at college. She took us under her wing, opened up her home, and really showed us how to pray. I can honestly say that Mother Davis was our teacher, and we were her students.

Mother Davis lived her life listening to the Spirit. She could quickly pick up on people and whether they were having a difficult time in life. I knew she was the perfect person to introduce to my roommate, Brad, because he was struggling but wouldn't talk about it. I told my friends, "Let's take him to Mother Davis, so she can get him in line."

So one Friday night, we took Brad over to Mother Davis's house. We were all sitting together in a circle in the room and Mother Davis said, "All right, let's pray." Each time we came to her home, Mother Davis would go around the circle and encourage each person. We were on the edge of our seats, waiting for her to get to Brad. We just knew she was going to let him have it. She looked at Brad straight in the eyes, and we all thought, *This is gonna be good.*

She began: "You're a mighty man of God. You're powerful. You're going to be amazing. God is going to continue to work on you."

We all just looked at each other, our mouths gaping open, all of us thinking the same thing: *Whoa! Mother Davis is a little off today. She isn't really seeing in the Spirit right now.*

That night, we took Brad back to the dorm, and then went back to her house. When we got there, Mother Davis immediately told us, "I know what you guys were doing. You brought that young man here thinking I would blast him. I saw in him what you see. But when you see a teaspoon of good in someone, it's best to magnify the teaspoon of good instead of the almost-full glass of bad. And when you're close to God, you look for the good rather than the bad."

I told you Mother Davis was a spiritual woman.

That night, this woman of God taught me that I wasn't as close to God as I thought I was. When we're chasing after God, we start to see what no one else can see. We seek out the good in people. When God called Moses to speak to Pharaoh and lead the

Israelites out of Egypt, Moses told Him, "Please God, don't choose me, I've never been good with words. I stutter and stammer." And God essentially told Moses, "Don't you think I know that Moses? I understand you can't speak that well. But Moses, I made you that way, and I see in you what you don't see."

When you get closer to God, you start to see as He does. This is why we're able to preach the gospel to people the world rejects. This is why we have compassion on the poor, the hungry, and the lost. We see people as God sees them—His creation.

Just like God sees you as His precious jewel, He sees others the same way. Have you ever thought about that? We tend to apply Scripture to us, and that's wonderful. But the same scriptures you internalize also describe others you cross paths with every day. Yes, you are the apple of God's eye (Deut. 32:10). So is the homeless woman on the corner pushing the grocery store cart you drive by each morning. Yes, you are God's masterpiece (Eph. 2:10, NLT). So is the guy in your office who always challenges your ideas and tries to undercut you. Yes, you are God's treasured possession (Deut. 7:6). So is the spouse who has betrayed you.

Just like God sees you as His precious jewel, He sees others the same way.

I'll never forget the first time I started to get God's heart for others. I was pastoring under Pastor "Choco" Wilfredo De Jesús. My wife and I were the first black people in the mostly Puerto Rican church, and I was the first black pastor to preach at the church. I knew I'd been sealed at birth, that God had placed a call on my life. I knew Choco had anointed me as a pastor. I knew I was reading the Scriptures. But it wasn't until I started ministering at a local men's shelter that I began to see people as God sees them.

Choco gave me an assignment. He said, "John, I want you to go to this men's shelter every Thursday night and do a devotion for five to seven minutes. Then I want you to feed these homeless men in the shelter. And then you guys are going to make sandwiches, and you're going to get in a van and look for other homeless people and feed them."

So I did it, though somewhat unwillingly. And this was when things started to change because to me, preaching was standing behind a pulpit. I had organized this inner-city youth conference. I was flying all over the country preaching. Now, with this new assignment, I was climbing onto viaducts and handing out sandwiches every week. I was used to preaching in front of 3,000 people, and now I was in a shelter preaching to twenty homeless men. The first Thursday night, I remember thinking, *Okay, God, this is different.* But my heart was changing. I was becoming more concerned about the poor, about those who were lost. I found myself weeping for these people and their brokenness. My prayers began to change: *God, help me feed the hungry. Help me clothe the naked.*

My wife and I live in Chicago about seven to eight minutes from the area where we're building our new church facility. The Grand Crossing Community has dire needs. We refuse to move to the suburbs or live in a gated community. We want to live in the city where I preach and where we shepherd. We don't want to be distant from people but instead live among them and get the heartbeat of the land.

Today, I have an inner-city ministry at our church, something I hadn't really thought about before those Thursday nights. All kinds of people come through the door of this church. We have a food pantry where we feed families every week. In the summer months, we set up hot dog stands on street corners. We give out school supplies. We've rehabbed some homes in the community. Each person I cross paths with, I want to see as Christ sees. I want to see the masterpiece, the hidden treasure. And the only way I can see that is by looking through the eyes and heart of God.

Do you see people as God sees them? Do you have the heart of God? Or are you at least moving closer toward finding it? Being desperate for Jesus and pursuing His heart changes the way we see and respond to others.

Once you have that personal encounter, you want more. And the more you get of Him, the more He changes you. My grandmother always said, "Draw nigh to God, John, and He'll draw nigh to you." He that comes to God must first believe that He is—*here it is*—*a rewarder* (see Heb. 11:6). Like I said earlier, when you diligently seek Him, He will fill you.

I think the thing that's hardest for some people is that they want immediate change. They want to see instant transformation. But just like I said in chapter 7, as we talked about overcoming spiritual maturity, change is a process. Just keep coming closer. Keep walking. Keep chasing.

Seeing God's Word and Power Unleashed

Often, following God's heart for His people takes us to unfamiliar, sometimes dark, places, just like what happened when I began to feed the homeless. When our chase brings us to these seemingly difficult areas, we get to see Jesus show up in ways we couldn't even fathom. His Word becomes more real. Seeing His power is life-changing.

If you put me in a gated community in the suburbs, my ministry wouldn't be the same. I'm called to urban ministry. I have to see hope. In a dark and seemingly hopeless situation, the smallest light shines bright. In a sense, God and His redemptive work are easier to see in the dark places.

Few places feel as hopeless and as dark as Hong Kong, where an estimated 40,000 heroin addicts, 100,000 gang members, and an unknown number of prostitutes live. A British missionary named Jackie Pullinger knows the darkness of this city all too well, specifically a walled, drug-infested area called Hak Nam, which literally means *darkness* in Chinese. The narrow alleys are dark, even during the day. Police hardly ever set foot in the crime-ridden place.

> *In a dark and seemingly hopeless situation, the smallest light shines bright.*

"Behind these tawdry shops rose the ramshackle skyscrapers," Pullinger wrote about seeing Hak Nam for the first time in 1966. "We squeezed through a narrow gap between the shops and started walking down a slime-covered passageway. I will never forget the smell and the darkness, a fetid smell of rotten foodstuffs, excrement, offal, and general rubbish."[1]

As she walked the area, Pullinger came up with the idea of managing just one street, so she began distributing food, taking people to hospitals, and even intervening in gang fights on the streets. Today, she organizes weekly meetings in the roughest of Hong Kong's neighborhoods and offers shelters and rehabilitation to 200 addicts, prostitutes, streets kids, and gang members. In this dark place, Pullinger has seen God show His power in her life and in the lives of countless others as young men and women make decisions for Jesus.

In her autobiography, *Chasing the Dragon,* Pullinger wrote about Christopher, who, on the cusp of becoming a member of the violent, Mafia-like gang Triad, cut ties with the members, got a real job, turned his life around, and began helping Pullinger with her youth club. These kinds of unlikely transformation stories run throughout Pullinger's ministry.

"I have spent over half my life in a dark, foul-smelling place because I had a vision of another city in its place, and that city was ablaze with light," Pullinger wrote in her 1989 book, *Crack in the Wall: Life and Death in Kowloon Walled City.* "There was no more crying, no more death or pain. . . . I had no idea how to bring this about, but with 'visionary zeal' [I] imagined introducing the Walled City people to the one who could change it all: Jesus."[2]

Because she followed God's heart for Hong Kong's forgotten forty-nine years ago, this woman has had the privilege of seeing God's Word and His power unleashed through her. She is blessed.

I get that. At New Life, I've seen His power to change lives that you would never expect to change. I've seen His Word truly manifested in people. Jeremiah 33:6 talks about the promise of restoring His people from the Babylonian exile: "Nevertheless, I will bring health and healing to it; I will heal my people and will let them enjoy abundant peace and security." The Bible says it's the sick who need a physician. I have had the privilege of watching God bring broken people health and healing. I've seen Him give them abundant peace and security.

In our church, young men come in who were drug dealers. People arrive straight from prison. We have a young man who works in our office. He's in his thirties and, until he came to us, had never worked a job a day in his life. He'd dropped out of high school and had only been involved in illegal activity. So we were the first to give him a job. We sent him to school to learn how to read and write.

Until coming to us, he had never been outside the city, just stuck in his community. One of the greatest things for me was inviting this young man to a leadership conference in Arizona, putting him on a plane, and taking him to restaurants—I got the opportunity to pay forward my time with Elder Willie James Campbell who taught me so much about life and what it was to be a man.

Here's someone who lived his life on the streets, and now he works full time in a supervisory position here at our church. Now he's traveled. Now he's a witness. Someone in his family invited this young man to our church, and we've seen several of his family members join. Christ used the church to expose him to the true life found in Him.

I remember the day a young lady came to meet with me at the church and said, "Pastor Hannah, I work at a gentlemen's club." I told her, "Okay, keep coming to church. Just keep coming because I believe if you have this encounter, God will spark in you a desperation for true life that's going to change how you live." Today, she has a full-time career. Her life has changed. Another lady here at the church came to me saying, "I'm an alcoholic. I drank for thirty-plus years, and I had lost everything. But I came to this church, and to God be the glory I'm getting my life back!" She's not drinking now. She's back working. She now has her own apartment.

When we trust Him to guide us into unfamiliar and sometimes uncomfortable places, He continues to give us glimpses of His power and kingdom on earth, and that, my friend, will keep us going in this life. That will keep us chasing toward His glory.

Changed From the Inside Out

It might sound a little odd, but I believe our desperation changes our outward appearance. I say that because I've seen it, in my own life and in the lives of countless others. I have watched broken and lost people change from the inside out.

When you're desperate for Jesus—and you know that He has a purpose for your life—He transforms you into who He has called you to be, whole and complete, inside and out.

Think about it: when Moses came down from Mount Sinai with the two tablets of the covenant law, Scripture says his face was *radiant* "because he had spoken with the LORD" (Ex. 34:29). His face shone so brightly that he had to put a veil over his face each time he came from speaking with God. Being in the presence of God literally changed his countenance. When you're desperate for Jesus—and you know that He has a purpose for your life—He transforms you into who He has called you to be, whole and complete, inside and out.

When I meet people and I share my story of coming from poverty, growing up in the "projects," they often say, "Man, you don't look like you grew up in the inner city. You don't look like you came from that past." When you crave God, you never look like what you came out of. He changes you, literally, in your process. The more you crave Him, the more you seek Him, the more you desire Him—the more He begins to transform you. As we're refined, the impurities, the dross, are removed and He begins to surface.

Now, don't get me wrong. I'm not saying that chasing after God is like a divine diet. You're not going to meet God and drop fifty pounds the next day. But I am saying that when you truly chase after Him, you begin to make better decisions that affect your spirit, mind, and body. First Corinthians 6:19 says that our bodies are "temples of the Holy Spirit, who is in you, whom you have received from God." He commands us to take care of our temples. Being changed from the inside out is a result of our obedience to Him.

You might have known someone who was at one time entrenched in darkness and addiction and then encountered Jesus and made Him Lord of their life. The more intense their chase, the more they began to look different physically. Something beautiful and redemptive happens when we come out of darkness and into light.

Vision Fulfilled

As I've continued to chase after Jesus, I've seen God fulfill my vision, my destiny. The fruit of a life of desperation changes us—and invites us in to take part in His story.

When I planted New Life Southeast in 2004, we started out with twenty-five people. We held a Bible study for seven months in a church every Thursday night and eventually moved to Sunday morning worship services in a facility that could hold 300 people. We continued to grow, moving from one place to another to accommodate the growth. I remember the day I saw a line of people waiting to get into the service. You would've thought we were a night club. I knew God was fulfilling my vision. To God be the glory!

The hand of God was on our ministry. People began to tithe into it. We bought a church building that could seat 1,100 people and kept our normal schedule of three services. And again, the line of people waiting to get into the service wrapped around the corner. So we rented another building around the corner of the church that could seat 300 people. To handle the overflow, we put up a video screen and streamed the service.

One Sunday, just eight months of being in that building, I was about to preach and saw a line of people in the foyer. I told someone, "We need to send these people to the overflow building."

"Overflow is full," he said.

"So what are we going to do with all these people?" I asked.

"They'll have to go home," he said.

Hearing that, I began to weep. And that's when God said to me, *Are you committed to a building, or are you committed to Me?*

That day, I started looking for a larger place to rent. Currently, we rent space in a 3,000-seat facility, and we hold three services. So every Sunday, we're able to minister to about 9,000 people, and then we stream our services into overflow areas so that those who can't get into the building can watch, too.

I thought that my vision had been fulfilled until one day I realized God had more. He does that. When we continue toward the prize, He blesses us, and when we take care of and multiply what He has given us, He gives us more. It's a biblical principle that Jesus illustrates in three parables. In one of those stories, the parable of the bags of gold (Matt. 25:14–30), a master gives five bags of gold to one of his servants, two bags to the second servant, and one bag to the third servant. After a long time, the master returns and asks each servant to account for what he did with his gold. The servants with five and two bags each doubled their amounts while the servant with one bag dug a hole and hid his in the ground. He had nothing to show for what he had received, yet he thought he had done a great job. Instead, the master condemned his lack of faithfulness.

But to the faithful servants who multiplied the treasure, he said: "Well done, good and faithful servant! You have been faithful with a few things; I will put you in charge of many things. Come and share your master's happiness" (v. 23)! Don't miss the reward they received: the commendation of their master; more to oversee; and an invitation to share in their master's joy.

In the same way, God entrusted me with 25 people, then 300, then 1,100 and so on. Now, our church is breaking ground on a 125,000-square-foot facility right in the heart of the urban community.

It's a vision four years in the making. One morning on my way to prayer, I was driving down the street and the Lord said to me, *Begin to buy every vacant home on the side of the street.* It took us four years, but our church now owns free and clear every piece of land and every house, as well as a factory, on three blocks. We paid cash for each one—no debt. The new building will be set up like a performing arts center. We will be able to seat 4,000 people at one time and meet the needs of people in the community. We can feed 300 people in the lobby, which I always say will eventually get them to the altar—all of this happening out of one building that God has given us!

We are literally inviting people into God's vision for our church and, more importantly, His vision for their lives. I saw this all happening way before we even planted New Life Southeast. When I was at New Life under Pastor Choco, he told me he would "plant me" one day. I was preaching at this church, living in this Puerto Rican neighborhood, and I remember praying, *God, if this is You, begin to send my friends and my leaders to where I am, so that I can build my team right here.* And my phone began to ring with friends telling me, "The Lord told me to come wherever you are. Where are you?" One by one, different friends and leaders began to come where I was, so they could see what I was seeing and get the same God-given vision and heartbeat for His people.

As we run for the prize and desperately seek to know Him, He reveals our destiny. Ultimately, His vision becomes our vision.

So That Others Will See

The fruit of our desperation is quite the reward: the privilege of seeing others the way God sees them; seeing His power and Word unleashed on earth; being changed from the inside out; and being used to fulfill His vision. But if we stop there, I'm afraid we've missed the point.

You see, anything God does is for His glory. When He moves in our lives, it's so that others can see His glory. His glory is not to be kept in. It's not for selfish means. If God has you at a place in life where you are desperate for Him, He's putting you there to bring about change in both you and others. He's putting you there to glorify Him.

It's almost like you ran someplace, and you encountered something so awesome that the first thing you want to do is go back and invite everyone to come see what you've seen, to encounter what you've encountered. I think of the woman at the well who met Jesus. After her conversation with Him, the Bible says she ran into town and said, "Come, see a man who told me everything I ever did. Could this be the Messiah?" Eventually, a revival started in the town.

> Many of the Samaritans from that town believed in him because of the woman's testimony, "He told me everything I ever did." So when the Samaritans came to him, they urged him to stay with them, and he stayed two days. And because of his words many more became believers. (John 4:39–41)

Many people became believers because of that woman. Once she experienced Jesus, she wanted *everyone* to experience Him. It wasn't enough to just know His power and keep it to herself. That's how the kingdom is advanced. A life of desperation for Jesus spreads like wildfire.

One of the greatest prayers I've ever read comes from 2 Chronicles 1:7–10 when God asked Solomon, "What do you want?" Solomon said something so powerful. He didn't ask for fame or riches. He prayed, "Lord, teach me how to go in and out among your people." That's a powerful prayer because everybody is so different, and how you conduct yourself around one person is not necessarily the most effective approach with someone else. That's discernment. You need that. The Bible says that Satan is slick. And if possible, he'll trick the very elect. You have no choice but to consistently pray for the gift of wisdom and discernment to most effectively reach and engage others.

This reminds me of what Paul wrote about being able to talk to the Gentile, the Roman, and the Jew:

> Though I am free and belong to no one, I have made myself a slave to everyone to win as many as possible. To the Jews I became like a Jew, to win the Jews. To those under the law I became like one under the law (though I myself am not under the law), so as to win those under the law. To those not having the law I became like one not having the law. To the weak I became weak, to win the weak. I have become all things to all people so that by all possible means I might save some. (1 Cor. 9:19–21)

Then he wrapped up the whole thing, saying why he did all this, what motivated his actions. Make sure you get this. Paul said: "I do all this *for the sake of the gospel*, that I may share in its blessings" (1 Cor. 9:23, emphasis mine).

God leaves nothing to chance. He warns us upfront that He's a jealous God. Whatever He has promised you, whatever miracles He performs in your life, He wants the glory from it. Friend, you must understand that anything God does for you or anything He works out in you, He does it to take you someplace that's about not only you but others as well. When God brings blessings, others around you are blessed as well, and ultimately He is glorified. What was God's command to the children of Israel? *"Remember Me. Remember My blessings. Keep Me in the center. Keep My commands."* Check out His commands in Deuteronomy 8 as they prepared to enter the land God had promised to them:

> Remember how the LORD your God led you all the way in the wilderness these forty years, to humble and test you in order to know what was in your heart, whether or not you would keep his commands. (Deut. 8:2)

> Be careful that you do not forget the LORD your God, failing to observe his commands, his laws and his decrees that I am giving you this day. (Deut. 8:11)

> But remember the LORD, your God, for it is he who gives you the ability to produce wealth, and so confirms his covenant, which he swore to your ancestors, as it is today. (Deut. 8:18)

Each week, Pastor Choco and I meet for accountability, and we always tell ourselves "to God be the glory" for the things He's doing in our ministries. We both lead large churches, and our ministry platforms continue to grow. Choco and I regularly remind ourselves that this is not about us. We want to make sure we give God the glory and do not believe the hype.

So even when I look around my church, and I see what God is doing, and I walk through the land that God has given us, I want to take no credit. None. Part of my desperation is to give Him glory. My desperation is that if anyone looks at me or at our church and what we're doing that God be glorified—not me.

When we start to look at ourselves, then we take our eyes off of Him and fail to give Him the glory. We can't take His credit. We must invite others to "come and see."

CHAPTER 10

STAYING DESPERATE

F ew people knew the names Dave Meyer, Jim Grove, Mike Johnson, and Kathy Goodwin before April 21, 2014. Few know them now. But the iconic photo of these four men and women carrying a wounded runner to the finish line of the Boston Marathon, one year after the tragic bombing, became the international symbol for the 118th historic race in Bean Town.

Meyer was the first to see the struggling runner visibly experiencing all the signs of physical exhaustion: shaking arms, wobbly legs, barely able to stand. The two runners were approaching mile twenty-six when Meyer saw the runner's legs about to give out. Soon, he caught up with the man and wrapped the runner's arm around his left shoulder.

"I was having a terrible race. At that point, my time didn't make any difference to me," Meyer told the *Washington Post.*

"I knew how important it was that I finish. So I knew it was important that he finish."[1]

But with no energy left in the runner and Meyer's strength waning, the hope of them both finishing began to fade. Meyer was about to give up when another runner, equally determined to finish the race, appeared. Like Meyer, Jim Grove also was having a terrible race. At the twenty-six-mile marker, Grove saw the runner struggling to finish and then watched as Meyer grabbed his arm and held him up. Grove caught up with the two men and grabbed the runner's other arm. At this point, Meyer and Grove wrapped the injured runner around their shoulders and slowly kept moving toward the finish line.

But carrying someone else when they had already run twenty-five miles proved difficult. Grove started to think they wouldn't make it when Mike Johnson and Kathy Goodwin showed up. Seeing the three men struggling, Johnson grabbed the runner's right leg while Goodwin grabbed the left leg. As the team of four came together—each one resolved that this injured runner would finish the race—the crowd of thousands of spectators roared with applause.

Suddenly, just a few hundred feet away from the finish line, the runner cried out, "Let me walk it. Let me walk across the finish. I need to finish."[2] As the crowd continued to cheer, the four runners set him down and each finished the race on his or her own, including the injured runner.

Just like this runner, sometimes on the road to desperation we have to let people carry us, especially when our legs have given out and we have nothing left to give. Sometimes, people will spot us struggling and will silently come alongside us to help. At other times in our lives, we'll need to humble ourselves and ask for help to stay desperate. Why do you think Paul tells us to "encourage one another and build one another up" (1 Thess. 5:11, ESV)?

Don't fool yourself. No one stays strong all the way to the finish line without others running alongside them, sometimes carrying them. Even Jesus' legs gave out on the way to the cross. And don't miss this! When we

Staying desperate is about being dependent on God and the people He places in our paths.

do try to walk or run the race all by ourselves, we rob people of the opportunity to be part of the story that God is writing. Think about the impact on the life of Simon of Cyrene from Africa who was picked out of the crowd to carry Jesus' cross—especially after news of the resurrection began to spread. Some biblical scholars believe that Simon (identified as Simeon called Niger in Acts 13:1) went on to become a leader in the church of Antioch. God had a plan for the African man, just as He has a plan for the people in your life who come alongside you.

Staying desperate is about being dependent on God and the people He places in our paths. It is the vulnerable place where weakness and the strength of God and the people He brings into our lives converge.

Ask for Accountability

Who in your life is asking about your soul and still loves you regardless of your response? We may think we have substantial relationships, especially in this age of social media-driven friendships, but just because we surround ourselves with people doesn't mean we have true community. Until we have people in our lives to whom we can come to with our deep hurts and lay out our guts before them knowing they'll walk with us, we don't have authentic accountability. And trust me, to stay desperate for Jesus and stay on this chase, you need accountability. You need to be able to say to someone or to a group of confidants, "This is where I am. This is what hurts." That kind of transparency is so necessary.

No one really likes fakeness in people, but I hate it. However, I'll be the first to say that unfortunately, sometimes the church can fuel a certain degree of fakeness—when, for example, the church community is an unsafe place where you fear being honest because judgment from others is sure to ensue. When you're afraid to lay your heart bare because someone will look down on you.

I get that. Church community can be that way. So you might need to look for biblical accountability outside your church. Just make sure you have it. I've seen so many leaders fall because they had no accountability. We can't stay desperate without it. This is where prayer comes in. Sometimes, we have to cry out in desperation for these kinds of relationships. I believe that when you ask Him, God will send you people you can be honest with and develop personal accountability.

I say this because I've had this kind of accountability ever since Edward Christian came into my life. God has always brought me the right people. I prayed for true accountability, for people who wouldn't let me get away with anything and wouldn't sugarcoat reality. Whatever's going on in my life, I have someone I can talk to about it. That's the honest to God truth. When Anna and I have gone through hard times in our marriage, I've had people in my life I could just sit with and share what was going on. I still have people either on my staff, or pastor friends, to whom I can go to and be honest with and really lay out my heart.

I'm always amazed at how the Holy Spirit works to bring people together. I was at a conference when a young man walked up to me and handed me his card. In the days after, I just kept hearing God say, *You need to call this young man.* So I did. Turns out he was a pastor who was in a very bad marriage and was about to get involved in some unhealthy habits. Before the conference, the Holy Spirit began to deal with him, and he prayed, *God, send me help! Send me help. I don't want to do this.*

The first or second time we met, I learned what my assignment was in his life, why I had sensed God telling me to call him. We sat at lunch, and the whole time the Holy Spirit was saying to him, *Okay, you asked for help; here it is, sitting in front of you. Lay it out.* This man gutted himself: "These are my struggles. This is where I'm falling short. This is what's going on in my house." And without so much as an eye wince I told him, "Okay. Let's go. You ready?" And I grabbed him like Edward Christian had grabbed me and walked him through very, very difficult and challenging times in his life. James 5:16 tells

> *Trust God. If you want true accountability, ask for it.*

us that honest, transparent relationships like this are powerful: "Therefore, confess your sins to one another and pray for one another, that you may be healed. The prayer of a righteous person has great power as it is working" (ESV).

To teach this young pastor some of the things Edward Christian and Elder Campbell had taught me, I had to hold this young pastor close like a son. He asked for help. That's key. I asked for help and got Edward Christian, Willie James Campbell, Mother Davis, Choco, and many others.

Trust God. If you want true accountability, ask for it. He will bring those people into your life. I firmly believe that's the *only way* we're going to stay on this pursuit of true life.

Keep Looking for God's Fullness

As much as Moses talked to God and was around Him, in Exodus 33:18, Moses told God, "Show me Your glory." In other words, let me see a side of You that I haven't seen yet. Moses never got to the point where he thought he had "arrived" in his relationship with his Creator. So why would we? We maintain our desperation when we long to encounter and experience the fullness of God.

In this Christian walk, there are parts of God we still have not encountered. There will always be another level, another chamber, that He hasn't opened to you yet. It's almost like someone walking you through his mansion, but he doesn't let you see it all at once. Instead, he reveals it to you room by room, and each one is more beautiful than the one before.

Think about the Scripture verses you've read. How many times have you looked at something and then the next year read the same verse and saw something you never saw before? It's the same passage, but your eyes and your spirit pick up something you didn't previously get. The Holy Spirit is revealing something new to you that, most likely, is extremely relevant for whatever you're walking through at that point. That's the way it is with God. We can say to Him, "Show me Your glory. Show me a side of You I've never seen before."

I've been reading my Bible for thirty-plus years now, and I'm still amazed at what He continues to show me through His Word. Every time I read, every time I research, He has a way of adding special seasoning to the same meal. I see something I've never seen before, especially now being in this pastoral seat. I preach from a whole other place.

Before this year, I never really thought about what I talked about in chapter 5—the fact that Jesus never went after Judas after he betrayed Him but instead stayed at the table with the eleven who would carry the church. This year, God gave me that revelation because I was crying about someone who had left our church. I didn't like the way he had exited or some of the things he was saying after he left. But there was a check in my spirit: *Stop, John! Why are you crying over this one? You need to focus on these still at this table and feed them. Don't worry about Judas.*

When you're desperate for Jesus, He gives you fresh revelation for what you're going through right now. In whatever situation you face, God will give you a fresh word for what you're dealing with—if you're in His Word and listening to His Spirit.

Those new discoveries and fresh insights are part of chasing after Him. Our pursuit of Jesus should never be boring. Chasing after Jesus is an adventure like no other. I love how Romans 8:15–17 (*The Message*) describes our pursuit:

> This resurrection life you received from God is not a timid, grave-tending life. It's adventurously expectant, greeting God with a childlike "What's next, Papa?" God's Spirit touches our spirits and confirms who we really are. We know who he is, and we know who we are: Father and children. And we know we are going to

get what's coming to us—an unbelievable inheritance! We go through exactly what Christ goes through. If we go through the hard times with him, then we're certainly going to go through the good times with him!

I like that idea of being "adventurously expectant," like an excited child asking his father, "What's next Daddy?" As we pursue our Father through prayer, the Word, and our community, we encounter more of who He is. We serve a God whose dimensions and depths are unfathomable. And if that was how the story ended, it would still be majestic. But thankfully His (and our) story doesn't end there. We serve a God who continually invites us in to seek out His dimensions, to dive into His depths, and ultimately to partake of His fullness. Glory be to God!

Staying Desperate Despite Personal Challenges

As we begin to wrap up this journey, I want to focus in on some especially difficult times when staying desperate for Jesus and continuing to chase after Him may sound completely overwhelming. I certainly don't have all the answers, but I want to at least equip you with some insights I and others have received along the way.

WHEN HE SAYS YOU CAN'T HAVE IT . . .

When you desire something so badly, like kids or marriage, and it's just not given to you, how do you stay desperate? Anna and I desperately wanted children. We wanted to be parents so badly. We were about to put our hands on it and attempt to make it happen when Anna said, "Let's stop. Let's just go with what's best—what God's will is." It was a difficult decision for both of us.

In hindsight, I'm glad we didn't put our hands on it. I understand now why we don't have children. If we had children, I could see where it would be a greater demand on our time. And if I had children, I would probably be just a little bit reluctant about living in the city. I know the power of education and surroundings.

We serve a God who continually invites us in to seek out His dimensions, to dive into His depths, and ultimately to partake of His fullness.

Something I learned through this is that you have to be comfortable with the fact that He knows what is best for your life, even though it may look different than what you expected and may not be what you desire at all. Even if you don't necessarily see it in the short term, you'll likely understand it later. We have to submit to God's perfect will, though it may hurt deeply. It's like the refiner placing the crucible in the flame because he understands the process and knows the outcome.

I may not always understand God's will—He gave us no promises we would—but I do know the God who's calling the shots. And I know He gets me and loves me despite my sin. I know He's all-powerful. I know He gave His most precious Son for a relationship with me, and that He wants to use my life to glorify Him. And that, friend, gives me confidence to trust my creator and Savior and to keep chasing even when I may not understand His ways—even when He says I can't have it.

How do you maintain the chase when you're physically weak and your body and mind don't function like they once did? For years I suffered from debilitating headaches, so I get it. Staying focused on Him instead of how badly you feel becomes quite difficult.

I remember when my grandmother was first diagnosed with cancer. Before she ever took a treatment, she took God's Word seriously and, believing that she would be healed, called for the elders in the church to lay hands on her. She called the pastor to the hospital, and he laid hands on her. And she was healed. She put her clothes on and walked out of that hospital proclaiming the miracle.

For seven years, my grandmother walked and lived her life. After seven years, the cancer resurfaced. I'll never forget this as long as I live. I went to her room and was talking to her, asking, "Granny, how do you feel?" She said, "You know, John, He let me walk seven years, and I asked God, 'Why did you let this thing come back?' He didn't give me an answer." Essentially, she was saying, "I don't get it now, but I'll get it later."

My grandmother used to sing the hymn "We'll Understand It Better By and By," and one of the verses says:

> *Trials dark on every hand, and we cannot understand*
> *All the ways of God would lead us to that blessed promised land,*
> *But He guides us with His eye, and we'll follow till we die,*
> *For we'll understand it better by and by.*[3]

In sickness, we have to know that while we might not understand it now, we'll get it later on one side of heaven or the other, and in the meantime He will guide us through the trials. My grandmother's words and how she approached life and death spoke volumes to me. Here was this woman lying there saying, "I still know He's God. I don't understand it. But I still know He's God."

Granny knew her Savior so intimately that she could ask, "Why did You let this cancer come back?" And when He didn't answer, she knew Him so deeply as to say, "You are God." May we all be so desperate to know our Savior in this way and for our spirits to be nourished and filled, even when our physical bodies (there's that flesh again!) betray us.

The Finish Line

"Behold, I see the heavens opened, and the Son of Man standing at the right hand of God. . . . Lord Jesus, receive my spirit" (Acts 7:56, 59, ESV).

Stephen's last few words right before he was stoned to death give us a solid reminder that the chase is not just about the chase. Ultimately, we're running to something. God has promised us that we have a finish line, what Paul calls the "heavenly prize": "I press on to reach the end of the race and receive the heavenly prize for which God, through Christ Jesus, is calling us" (Phil. 3:14, NLT).

At the end of this desperate chase is eternity with Jesus. Don't forget that. In fact, stay focused on it. Don't let your eyes stray from it. Remember all that God has done to save you and make you His heir. Remember everything He has given you—prayer, His Word, the people in your life—to stay desperate for Him and run toward the prize.

When God breathed life into the first man, Adam became a living soul, and he craved God. It is the God-nature of humanity. Unfortunately, we attempt to fill that craving with other things—drugs, alcohol, relationships, money, fame. But our eternal part craves the eternal God. Not only do you have the promise of eternity with Him, you were born for eternity with Jesus. God brought you onto this earth to glorify Him and one day bring you back to your eternal home with Him. Our God loves us so much. Don't ever forget that.

Friend, my prayer and hope for you is that you keep pressing on in this chase and that you confront any obstacles in your life that are keeping you from finding abundant and true life in Him. The finish line is worth it!

ENDNOTES

INTRODUCTION

1. http://www.jesuswalk.com/lessons/18_35-43.htm

CHAPTER 1

1. "As the Deer," lyrics by Martin J. Nystrom, 1983 Restoration Music Ltd.

CHAPTER 3

1. http://www.hopefortheheart.org/july-2013-letter-from-june-on-trials/

2. http://nymag.com/news/features/cancer-peter-bach-2014-5/index3.html

CHAPTER 4

1. http://www.alternet.org/story/149890/9_life-changing_inventions_the_experts_said_would_never_work

2. Ibid.

3. http://blog.genealogybank.com/amazing-inventors-thomas-edison-the-electric-light-bulb.html

4. Ibid.

5. http://www.nytimes.com/2002/02/24/nyregion/quotation-of-the-day-780197.html

CHAPTER 5

1. Stephen Dietz, *Dracula* (New York: Dramatists Play Service, Inc., 1996), 59.

2. http://biblehub.com/commentaries/luke/22-3.htm

3. Stoyan Zaimov, "Rwandan Genocide 20th Anniversary: Survivor Talks Forgiving the Man Who Murdered His Family," *The Christian Post* (blog post), April 6, 2014. http://m.christianpost.com/news/ rwandan-genocide-20th-anniversary-survivor-talks- forgiving-the-man-who-murdered-his-family-117436/

4. Ibid.

5. Ibid.

CHAPTER 6

1. Warren Wiersbe, *Angry People and What We Can Learn From Them. Living Lessons from God's Word* (Grand Rapids, MI: Baker Books, 2001), 3.

2. Aristotle, *Nicomachean Ethics,* trans. W. D. Ross. Book II.9. http://classics.mit.edu/Aristotle/ nicomachaen.2.ii.html

3. See *Pulpit Commentary* on Matthew 21 at http:// biblehub.com/commentaries/pulpit/matthew/21.htm

4. Natalie Angier, "Chronic Anger May Lead to Early Death," *Chicago Tribune,* 20 December 1990. http://articles.chicagotribune.com/1990-12-20/ news/9004150151_1_chronic-anger-early-mortality- hostile

5. J. Paul Reno, "Daniel Nash, Prevailing Prince of Prayer," (sermon), 1989. Posted at *Way of Life Literature,* 30 August 2012. http://www.wayoflife.org/index_files/daniel_nash_prince_of_prayer.html

6. Hitendra Wadhwa, "The Wrath of a Great Leader: How Martin Luther King, Jr., Wrestled With Anger," www.inc.com (blogpost), 21 January 2013. http://www.inc.com/hitendra-wadhwa/great-leadership-how-martin-luther-king-jr-wrestled-with-anger.html

7. Ibid.

CHAPTER 7

1. Simon Hart, "Usain Bolt disqualified from men's 100 metres final at World Athletics Championships in Daegu as fellow Jamaican Yohan Blake wins gold," *The Telegraph,* 28 August 2011. http://www.telegraph.co.uk/sport/olympics/athletics/8728032/Usain-Bolt-disqualified-from-mens-100-metres-final-at-World-Athletics-Championships-in-Daegu-as-fellow-Jamaican-Yohan-Blake-wins-gold.html

CHAPTER 8

1. William L. Kynes, "Dying to the Flesh," *Knowing & Doing* (Spring 2013), http://www.cslewisinstitute.org/Dying_To_the_Flesh_FullArticle

2. Arthur Tappan Pierson, *George Müller of Bristol* (London: Pickering & Inglis, 1899), 367. http://books.google.com/books/about/George_Müller_of_Bristol.html?id=EFbkOf1YoJQC

3. Quoted in Jim Luthy, "To Fast or Not to Fast, That Is the Question" (sermon), *Sermon Central,* March 2002. http://www.sermoncentral.com/sermons/to-fast-or-not-to-fast-jim-luthy-sermon-on-disciplines-fasting-44456.asp

4. https://scannedthoughts.wordpress.com/2010/03/29/the-12-apostles-skinned-stoned-crucified-and-beheaded/

5. Kynes, "Dying to the Flesh."

6. C. S. Lewis, *Mere Christianity* (New York: HarperOne, 2001), 63.

CHAPTER 9

1. Jackie Pullinger with Andrew Quicke, *Chasing the Dragon* (Ann Arbor: Servant Books, 1980), 36.

2. Jackie Pullinger, *Crack in the Wall: Life and Death in Kowloon Walled City* (London: Hodder & Stoughton, 1989), 16.

CHAPTER 10

1. Wesley Lowery, "The Story Behind That Boston Marathon Photo of Runners Carrying a Competitor Toward the Finish," *The Washington Post,* 22 April 2014. http://www.washingtonpost.com/news/post-nation/wp/2014/04/22/the-story-behind-that-boston-marathon-photo-of-runners-carrying-a-competitor-toward-the-finish/

2. Ibid.

3. Charles Albert Tindley, "We'll Understand It Better By and By" (No. 525) in *United Methodist Hymnal* (Nashville, TN: United Methodist Publishing House, 1989).

ACKNOWLEDGMENTS

T o God, my *everything*, who has given me *amazing* favor that has exceeded my expectation, I am forever grateful that You chose me to be Your servant, and I count it a privilege to be whom You created me to be. It is my prayer that You receive *the glory, honor, and praise* out of my life. I'm in love with You forever!

To the Salubris Resources team, thank you for believing in me and my story. Steve and Susan Blount, I appreciate the opportunity to be a voice in the growing arsenal of authors who are helping to make disciples and equip the church. Thanks also to my editor, Lindy Lowry, for helping tell my story and the story of New Life Southeast. And thank you to Plain Joe Studios for the cover design.

To Anna, my God-given *gift* . . . we have been together since 1993, and every day I ask God to let me spend my life with *only* you. You are my wife, my friend, my lover, and my soul mate. *I love me some Anna Hannah!*

To my close family and friends, I would be a fool to call names but each of you know who you are and what you mean to me. You are my village that knows me from the inside out. Many of you were there before "pastor" was attached to my name and have loved me before the crowd. When the spotlight goes out and the crowd becomes thin, you are the ones I call my family and friends.

To the pastors and leaders of New Life that help me carry the cross, you make what I do easy. Words could never express my appreciation. God sent each of you to me and for that I say, *Thank You, Jesus!* The stage is big, but each of you has a special place in my life and my heart. I'm excited about our future together.

To the brotherhood of senior pastors that I laugh, pray, study, and have serious conversation with, I'm in awe of how God brought us together. God knew that I needed brotherhood, and He divinely connected us. Let's continue to cover one another like brothers do!

To the three men who have left their thumbprint on my life and helped me become the man of God I am today: the late Edward Christian, Bishop Willie James Campbell, and Pastor Wilfredo De Jesús. When I look at my life, I can point to each area that God used each of you to pour into me. Thanks for pulling me close!

To the members of New Life Southeast, please know that I'm a happy man because of you. I count it such a privilege that you allow me to feed you, lead you, and serve you. Never think that I take your love, prayers, and support for granted. I say to you as I say all the times standing in front of you, *"New Life, I love you! Now give me a hug!"*

ABOUT THE AUTHOR

John F. Hannah exemplifies "a man after God's own heart," shepherding the approximately 19,000 members who participate in New Life Covenant Church—one of the fastest growing churches in the U.S. With an uncanny ability to reach those who have never stepped foot in church, as well as restore those who may have been hurt in past religious experiences, he is affectionately known as the "pastor of second chances and the unchurched."

Hannah's vibrant personality and his willingness to go to any length to illustrate God's Word combine to engage the people who attend New Life's Sunday and Thursday services. His capacity to maintain a high energy level in the services stems from his many years ministering to youth throughout the country. He served as a youth pastor of a local church for many years, and year after year doors opened to evangelize America's youth. Locally, he served as executive director of the Inner-City Youth Spring Break Conference (IYSBC), which grew exponentially under his leadership. Perhaps it's his experience working with IYSBC and his past experience as a Cook County juvenile probation officer that continue to drive his undying love for changing young hearts and lives through Christ. Currently, more than 74 percent of his church population is under the age of thirty-five.

Growing up in Chicago and having worked with the city's youth in church and secular arenas also compels Hannah's ongoing concern for the city and its ills and needs. He continues to refuse suggestions to move the New Life campus from the inner city to other Chicago areas deemed safer. Instead, New Life Southeast operates two multi-million dollar facilities on the south side of Chicago, soon to be joined by the church's new home, known as The Temple. At any given service at New Life Covenant, it isn't unusual to find a millionaire sitting next to an ex-addict. The congregation's diversity, sense of family, and the presence of God make New Life a church committed to serving God and the surrounding community.

In addition to his growing platform at New Life, Hannah is also known throughout Chicago for his voice. For more than thirteen years, he hosted the city's number one-rated gospel radio program, "The John Hannah Morning Show," and in 2012 earned a Stellar Award for Gospel Radio Announcer of the Year.

In 2007, Hannah added "author" to his repertoire. His first book, *What to Do While You're Waiting,* was birthed after his own experience waiting for God's plan to unfold in his life. His second book, *Desperate for Jesus,* challenges readers to overcome the obstacles in their lives to find true life. Hannah is married to Anna, who serves alongside him at New Life Covenant. Married in 1993, the Hannahs live and minister in Chicago.

FOR MORE INFORMATION

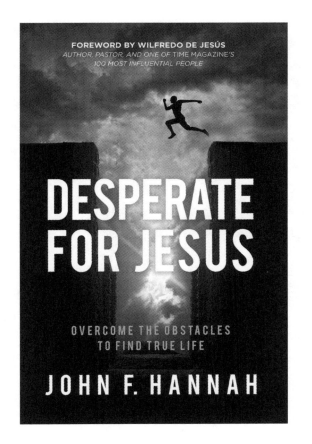

FOR MORE INFORMATION ABOUT THIS AND OTHER VALUABLE
RESOURCES VISIT WWW.SALUBRISRESOURCES.COM